P9-CMP-516

FATHERS
WITHOUT
PARTNERS

FATHERS
WITHOUT
PARTNERS

A Study of
Fathers and the Family
after Marital Separation

KRISTINE M. ROSENTHAL
HARRY F. KESHET

ROWMAN AND LITTLEFIELD
Totowa, New Jersey

To Our Families
Richard, Lisa and Jeffrey Rosenthal
Jamie Kelem Keshet, Matthew Finkelstein,
Ezra and Daniel Keshet

Copyright © Rowman and Littlefield 1981

First published in the United States of America, 1981, by Rowman and Littlefield,
81 Adams Drive, Totowa, New Jersey.

Distributed in the U.K. and Commonwealth by
George Prior Associated Publishers Limited
37-41 Bedford Row
London WC1R 4JH, England

Library of Congress Cataloging in Publication Data

Rosenthal, Kristine M   1933–
    Fathers without partners.

    Bibliography: p.
    Includes index.
    1. Father and child—Case studies.
2. Divorced fathers—United States—Case studies.
3. Single parents—United States. I. Keshet, Harry F., 1940–   joint author. II. Title.
HQ756.R67   306.8′7   80–11281
ISBN 0–8476–6281–0

Printed in the United States of America

Table of Contents

Preface

In the spring of 1975 I had a meeting scheduled with a colleague, Dr. Harry Keshet, to discuss research interests we had in common. At the time our interest was in the development of children in different types of families. On the day we were supposed to meet, Dr. Keshet phoned me sounding rather harassed and apologetic. It seemed that he had a five-year-old son whose care he shared with his divorced wife. School was letting out early that day, the babysitter could not come, and he was sorry but he would have to cancel the meeting.

Being divorced myself and having custody of three children, I was an old hand at juggling child care and work obligations. I suggested that we meet at my house instead of the office and that he bring along his son. My youngest was about the same age—they could keep each other entertained while we talked.

They came. The boys got along perfectly, and our conversation naturally drifted to the difficulties of fitting a work schedule, even as flexible and self-determined as that provided by teaching and research, to the needs of five-year-olds. Harry was a recently divorced father, who, himself a child of divorced parents, was determined to preserve a close relationship with his son and, as a person trained in the science of human relations, he knew that the reality of such a relationship depended on daily contact.

A great deal goes on in the life of a small child every day. Any parent who has had occasion to take a trip away from his or her family for even just a week or two knows how changed small children can seem after such an absence. An adult or a teenager can bring one up on their inner and outer state when visited at intervals; a small child can't.

Harry and his wife agreed on a split-week schedule. Each took full responsibility during the time that Matthew was with them. It gave Jane the time she needed to develop her career, thus making her better able to create a full life for herself and to share the financial burdens of Matthew's upbringing.

I was very interested by that arrangement. My own situation was quite different. My marriage had dissolved some four years previously, and I had not heard of such innovative solutions at the time. Just to prove the statistics right, I, too, was a child of divorced parents, and in my early childhood I had spent every other Sunday dutifully and pleasantly with my father. I remember him only vaguely, as the visits grew more infrequent after my mother remarried. My father died when I was a teenager, and we never had a chance to reestablish our relationship as adults.

At the time of my divorce I was already used to a routine of working and taking care of the children. It seemed quite improbable at the time that my ex-husband would be able to do the same. After all, he was a man and not used to such a double life. He never thought of trying it then, and I never expected him to. Still, he felt close to the children, took them on alternate weekends, vacationed with them for a month each summer, and was available by phone. He was not remarried, and was more involved with them than many other divorced fathers I knew.

During our discussion, Harry and I were struck by the similarities in our situation. We had both experienced the same feelings of alienation from coworkers who were easily available for meetings at odd times and colleagues who spent long evenings in the library, making such overtimes seem the expected norms of work. We had both experienced self-doubts: I wondering if it was really possible to have a full-time commitment to work that *I wanted* to do and still be an adequate mother as well; *he* wondering if as a man he could really undertake full responsibility for a child, even part-time. We shared, also, the discomfort when as parents we had to leave the transporting of children or baking of cookies to others, because our own time was limited.

Our interests were basically the same: we wanted to do the work which we liked and to take care of our children, and we were willing when necessary to be inconvenienced and limited, and to expend the extra energy to make it possible. Although I had always worked, weathering the disapproval of older family members and an occasionl acquaintance, my views had been recently reinforced by the women's movement. My situation ceased to be an isolated struggle. As career goals for women became encouraged, more women were available to me as coworkers and friends, and these women tended to understand my problems and were often willing to help out. Knowing many other women in the same situation, being able to avail myself of day-care facilities, and having the current supportive atmosphere all had become important to me.

This was less true for Harry. He knew few men who had child care responsibilities. Financial support for his ex-wife and children was all that was expected of a separated father. Few people understood or supported his decision to share child care. His lawyer was discouraging about attempting to arrange for joint custody. His coworkers wondered if his ex-wife ''made him do it,'' and the child's doctor, dentist and teacher were not sure if he was the ''right'' parent to talk to.

As social scientists we knew that we represented a growing phenomenon of single parenthood. We were, in fact, participants in a major social change. In 1976 there were 3.8 million separated persons and 7.2 million divorced persons. This represents double the numbers reported in the 1960 census. The most rapid increase in the divorce rate over the past ten years has been among men with college educations, although the largest number of divorced men can still be found among those with partial college educations. Seventeen percent of all children under eighteen live with one parent only. Three-fourths of those are living with a divorced parent. This parent is generally a mother. Only one child in ten lives with a divorced father. The total number of single parent families has increased threefold since 1960. (Pop. Bul. 1977).

The statistics stop there. Where are the fathers of the remaining nine-tenths of children of divorce? Are they lost to their children? How often do they see them? What input do they make into their children's lives?

It is generally predicted that the divorce rate will continue to rise and the number of single families will increase. 1977 population studies predict that as many as 45 percent of all children born in that year will spend some part of their growing years as members of one-parent families.

We have some information on the rates of default on child-support and alimony payments. Following divorce there is a progressive rate of default. Ten years after divorce, 79 percent of fathers of minor children have defaulted on child-support payments. We can assume that a father who is not keeping up with such payments is not coming around much. These are the men whose hopes of family life have turned into an embarrassment or a regret. Where do they go after they no longer share a house with their own children and the children's mother? What do they do? What does being a father mean to them after the divorce? How does a man who has shared his child's everyday life adjust to "visiting rights," and conversely, how does the man who only glimpsed his children at bedtime or yelled good night up the stairs at his wife's prompting, begin to share anything at all with them when even that much contact is no longer available?

Young children are the easiest to abandon. The family of a young child has only a short history. Six or seven years can be easily erased from an adult's life, the disruption healed over, new partners found, new commitments made. The five- or seven-year-old offspring can become little more than an uneasy reminder of temporary wrong turns of events. Young children make the greatest demands on the parents' time and energy just at the time when that parent is most intent on developing a career or a personal life. Yet these same young children are at their own most formative time, and the fathering they miss than can not be easily made up later when, as more manageable adolescents, they can be treated as acquaintances or guests.

Our decision to find out more about fathers of young children eventually developed into a research project. The first step was to ask men we knew if they would be willing to talk to us about their feelings and experiences in dealing with their children following separation. We were interested not only in their experiences as separated fathers, but also in the life histories that led up to the separation. What kinds of hopes and expectations did these men have for their future families as they themselves were growing up? We wanted to know just as much as they were willing to tell us: about their days of courting and early marriage, about what it felt like to be a father and what it feels like to be a man—anything at all which to them was relevant to their present situation.

Based on the insight we could gain from those life histories, we planned and designed a more structured, shorter interview which was then administered to a selected group of 129 men with children seven years old and under, who took care of those children anywhere from alternate weekends to full-time. Four of these case histories are presented in Chapter Two. We have changed only the names and minor details to protect the anonymity of our respondents.

We found that the men welcomed the opportunity to talk about their experiences. It was, for most, the only chance they had to talk about their feelings about child care. They allowed us to tape record long, open-ended interviews taking time from their work or sleep, reliving the painful first months of the separation, and the first happy moments of feeling confident and rewarded as a single parent.

Most men have little opportunity to share their feelings and express their uncertainties. As husbands or lovers, as fathers, as workers, men are expected to exude an air of confidence and self-assurance, even through the crises of their lives. So, as the objective researchers, not involved in any way that mattered in their daily lives, we were welcomed as listeners. We wanted to hear about their experience in their own words, in whatever sequence it seemed important.

Every man's experience was unique. Each man felt alone. For many of these men, trying to behave normally at work and appear strong and reliable to their children created an emotional strain difficult to share. We were often moved and always impressed by the sincerity of the feelings, by the depth of disruption that is created by a broken marriage, no matter how long the break was in the making or how welcome the final resolution.

Time would run out and we would come back again; usually three visits of two to four hours completed the session. All ten men shared their experience with us in this way. Some just wanted to be able to talk and maybe in the process put it all together for themselves. Others wanted our reassurance that they were doing the best they could, or that their lives were like those of other men. Still others were proud of how they have managed and happy to tell us about the solutions they had arrived at. Later we would go over those lengthy interviews, select common themes and begin to put together a questionnaire we would give to a greater number of men.

And so began a three-year collaboration—collaboration not just between the two authors, but one that included some one hundred and thirty men who talked with us, answered our questions, shared their experiences, and told us much about how the lives of men change when, willingly or reluctantly, with greater or lesser success, they undertake the pleasures and the burdens of single parenthood.

We hope that an account of these experiences can be interesting and useful to others who find themselves in that situation. We ourselves learned very much from it: about men, about children, about marriages and families. We learned that fathering means many things, that divorce need not mean an inevitable distancing of a father and his children. We learned that men can be part-time fathers and yet feel closer to their children and more knowledgeable about them than when they lived with them full-time as married men. We found men who were able to negotiate comfortably with their ex-wives about the well-being of their children and carefully avoid the conflicts which had destroyed the marriage. And we met men who juggled work lives, personal lives and parenthood and emerged to feel better, more whole humans for the difficulties they mastered.

Many social scientists have said that children need fathers. We have concluded that men need their children. It will be some time yet before the trend towards increased divorce rate slows down or reverses. In the meantime we can and perhaps should begin to view divorce not as a breakup of a family, but as a redefinition of it. Once a child is born to a man and a woman there is a connection between them which must be considered no matter how their life situation or their feelings about each other change. They have created a permanent family, and only its form can be negotiated. Who is to say that children who spend part of their time with a mother who loves and cares for them, and the other time with the father who is equally caring and competent, are in any less stable situation than children whose parents cohabit? It is very likely that children who have regular access to both parents, and a sense of the concern and caring that these parents have for them, are fully and adequately parented whether or not the parents are divorced. Such arrangements may present some practical difficulties, but they are not impossible. The men we interviewed represent different versions of the attempts at postdivorce parenthood. Some were more satisfying or more successful than others. Yet almost all of the men we spoke with said they now felt closer to their children than they did before the separation. They attributed that closeness to the fact that they were now more likely to be alone with their children and the time spent together was more intense and meaningful. Perhaps what the fathers have learned was that the breakup of the marriage did not have to diminish their input into their children's lives. The input was now actually more direct.

It is this direct relationship to a child that characterizes fathering outside the marriage. Perhaps it can tell us new things about what it means to be a father which can be applicable within a marriage as well. In presenting our findings we will let the fathers speak for themselves:

Since separation I have often wondered what is a good parent and more specifically, what is my relationship in regard to my children . . . ? It is almost as if the separation has given me cause to really wonder what is my role. The questions seemed new. You'd think having two children I would know all that. [A thirty-two-year-old father of two, a year after separation.]

The study reported in this book was supported by grants from the Rockefeller Foundation. We are especially indebted to Dr. Mary Kritz of the Rockefeller Foundation for her support and encouragement and to the fathers who shared their time and experience with us so candidly.

K.R.

A Father Speaks

When my parents split up I was sixteen, I remember having a sinking feeling in my stomach whenever I told my friends about the divorce. I felt ashamed and confused. Why couldn't the two people I loved stay together? I made a vow that if I married it would be forever and I would have a real family that stayed together.

My own marriage ended in divorce after eight years.

During those eight years my wife and I had a son. Now I realize that I put him through some of what I went through as a boy. But there is a difference, too. My wife and I settled on a shared custody arrangement, and I stayed close to my boy despite the divorce. Over the last five years I have experienced the joys and pains of part-time parenting. During the school year my son, Matt, spends half the week living in my home and half the week living with his mother. We divide Matt's vacations, holidays and summers between our two households.

This arrangement grew from my desire to be close with my son and from some painful memories of my past. When my parents separated, my father visited only occasionally. We weren't very close. I blamed him.

When I separated, I feared that I, too, would lose my son's

love and affection. Suddenly, I understood how my dad must have felt.

Finding a lawyer that would work for this half-time arrangement wasn't easy, though many lawyers gave lip service to father involvement. When I laid out my plan I ended up having to defend myself against the lawyer whom I sought to represent me. Most lawyers felt that my ex-wife should care for Matt and I should visit occasionally and pay the bills. Even some friends talked against "too much involvement" on my part. "How can you move him each week?" "It's not natural." "He'll suffer!"

For me, shared parenting seemed quite simple and obvious. I wanted to love and care for Matt and be part of his life as he grew up. I wanted him to know me as a real father, not just as a picture on the wall or a Santa Claus Daddy. Being a father meant being with Matt as much as possible. I couldn't accept the idea that the failure of our marriage meant I had to stop being an active and loving parent.

Being Married, Being a Father

Jane and I had met in college and we got married after I graduated. I was twenty-three and Jane was twenty-one. These were the sixties with the civil rights and antiwar movements sweeping across the nation. We joined in and worked for the changes we believed in.

There seemed to be very good reasons why our marriage should have lasted. We had similar backgrounds and had even grown up within two miles of each other. We were preparing for similar careers and often helped each other with our studies or our work problems. For us, a household meant sharing the chores. I more often cooked, shopped and did the laundry, while Jane more often cleaned, decorated and did the dishes. We both went to graduate school, worked and shared our earnings.

In hindsight, it is easy to see both our differences and our failures at learning to resolve them. I was the more distant emotionally; frequently, I didn't know when something was upsetting me or how to say what I felt. I avoided confrontations, then exploded. I liked quiet home things. Jane was more direct, more verbal, and she was quick to argue. She lived an active social life, was a joiner and enjoyed a large network of friends.

Matt was born after three years of marriage. It just seemed right to have a child. I was near the end of my studies, Jane had her graduate degree and was tired of working. We had some money saved and we both wanted a true family with children. After three months of vitamin E, queen bee jelly and temperature checks, Matt was conceived. We were excited, expectant parents, reading infant care books and taking natural childbirth classes at the local Y.

Matt's delivery seemed endless. Twenty hours of breathing, panting, yelling and pushing. Matt was fantastic with his long, chubby body and unbelievably big shoulders. Helping him get born, seeing him and holding him at birth filled me with wonder. I loved him immediately.

At first I wasn't too involved with caring for Matt. I felt that there wasn't much I could really do for him. Jane was breast feeding. They seemed inseparable, intense and interdependent. For over a year, Jane was engrossed with being a "good mother": she stopped working, stopped attending meetings, stopped going out and stopped her political activities. In contrast to Jane, I was the busy helper. I helped by changing Matt, bathing him, watching him, walking him, soothing him, playing with him. My energies also went into finishing graduate studies.

Breaking Up

The women's movement played a big role in changing both our marriage and my fathering activities. I believe that the women's movement has been and remains the most profound force shaping women and the relationship between the sexes. But I must say also that it acted as a catalyst in the breakup of our marriage. As an active participant, Jane found the impetus for forcing needed changes in our family lives. But she also found license to see all of her troubles, past, present and future, as stemming from sexism and male chauvinism. Whatever I did, from making breakfast to making love, she hastily labelled "sexist." Suddenly I became Jane's enemy. I was "The Man."

Breaking up was a painful time. We both said and did hurtful things to each other. I often felt bitter and reacted with feigned indifference to Jane's independence. Jane turned a deaf ear to my feelings and concerns. We became stones, hard and distant, rarely touching, opening up only to release sudden fury as our love and respect for each other dimmed.

During this time, I shared caring for Matt reluctantly. I imagined myself as a "super dad," working and caring for my kid. Many of our women friends praised me, while the men thought I was strange. I now realize, though I often felt ambivalent about my decision to share parenting, I felt closer to Matt than I had before. I knew him better and dealt with his changing needs and moods. I loved him more as I knew him more. In contrast, Jane and I grew more distant: we spent less time as a family with Matt. As our marriage fell apart, our battles took me away from Jane and toward our son. Matt became more important to me than Jane was.

We made a last-ditch effort to save the marriage: a new job and a new city. It failed. Instead of giving us both new energy, the move only showed me that we had little to build on. Our fights increased and I lost hope.

I felt very guilty and concerned about Matt. How was he taking our yelling and upsets? How could I help him when I was feeling so bad? I felt powerless to give him the kind of family life I wanted him to have. Was I hurting him in the same way that my dad had hurt me when he left? It made me cry.

Matt was three when Jane and I split up. Although Jane agreed to a shared custody arrangement, I still had my fears and questions. What did it mean to live apart from him? Would he want to be with me? How do you make an apartment feel like home? How do you make a child understand that you love him? What if the court declares that I was a bad person and gave him to Jane? How could I make lawyers and friends understand and help me? Besides dealing with the endless questioning, I encountered an unwelcome new reality.

I felt helpless, depressed and powerless. Doing the simplest things in my apartment or at work took great effort. My life suddenly seemed meaningless. I was living with strangers and not being with my family. I couldn't predict what would happen in the future. Everything just didn't seem "real"! My world was crumbling, and so was I.

To my surprise, taking care of Matt for part of each week helped me to get myself together. A three-year-old needs to be fed, bathed, played with, cared for, hugged and put to bed. This called for the basics, and the basics were just what I needed. He needed me, and I needed to be needed by my own child. Just having him around made the past connect with the present, and it even made the future seem less uncertain and scary.

The hardest times each week were taking Matt back to Jane's on Sunday mornings and picking him up again after day care on Wednesdays. When I took him to Jane it always felt as if he were leaving my life completely—as if he were suddenly going off to college at the age of three!

The hour before we'd have to leave was the hardest. Matt would get impatient. He'd put on all his winter clothes, talk about his mother and ask me over and over, was it time to go yet? Other times he'd want to stay with me and he'd cry as I got him ready to go. It wasn't any easier for me. Taking him back to Jane just reminded me of my failures, my losses and powerlessness. As if that weren't enough, Jane always wanted to chat. Had I paid the day-care bill? Did I know where the other red sock was? Would I like to hear about her new job? One time Matt ran to my car as I was leaving. He leaned on the car door and wept, "I don't want you to go. Stay here with me and Mom." I went home and stayed in bed for two days.

Finding an easy way to connect with Matt after not being with him took time and experience. When I first picked him up after day care I wanted to hug him a lot, talk with him about his day and discuss my plans for our time together. Matt wouldn't respond. He'd just sit and look out the window. I slowly learned that I couldn't be so intense. We needed a warm-up time. We'd go to a park and play ball, or I would push him on the swings. We'd go home and play a game of pick-up-sticks for a while. We needed something to bring us together slowly without talking about ourselves. I began to learn how to be close, and we became closer than we'd ever been. It helped that many things remained the same—bedtime continued to be as special as before. I read stories and sang, and Matt joined in with laughter as he always had done.

I also learned to be more in tune with Matt's feelings, to try to find out what his needs were and help him feel better. I began to trust my intuitions. I remember a time when Matt was miserable. He couldn't tell me what it was, but I could tell that he missed his mother. One phone call later all the tears and sadness had become smiles.

As a single parent I had to learn to be organized, a talent that I never possessed before. Jane had been a superb manager. She could orchestrate clothes, day care and entertainment with ease. Parenting, I found, was a lot more complicated than just being with Matt. I had to learn to fit together work, homemaking, child care and all the unanticipated challenges of being a parent. I began to plan and think about what was needed in advance. Going to the beach is a lot more fun when you don't forget to bring the kid's bucket and shovels and a change of clothes.

Relating with my Ex-Wife

When we first separated, Jane and I argued frequently. Jane would call me to ask for what seemed like husbandly tasks. Would I come over and fix the sink? What was my opinion about her job offer? I didn't want to be her husband. I refused, and we both felt upset. I felt even more upset refusing Jane's requests for help with Matt. Could I bring Matt back later on Sunday? Would I watch him on Tuesday after school instead of Wednesday? My saying no made Jane angry and her anger upset me. Slowly we learned to look elsewhere before asking each other for help.

We also used to argue about holiday schedules. I doggedly defended myself against what I felt at the time were Jane's unfair demands. Now I see that Jane wanted Matt as much as I wanted him and that my anger had covered my loneliness and loss. Our separation took away the family feeling of the holidays, and I missed it.

A significant event that changed our future negotiations occurred when Matt's day-care teacher reported that he had difficulties at school on the days when he changed households. Jane suggested that we change the schedule.

I refused. We discussed, argued, stopped talking to each other and got nowhere. Finally, we agreed to meet with a child guidance professional. Our counselor observed Matt at our homes, in school and in the clinic. She recommended that he stay with Jane on the school days and with me on weekends and one afternoon during the school week. I didn't like it, but I accepted it, and to my delight, Matt quickly felt happier in school and with each of us.

With guidance we could accept that we each had different styles of parenting, and we could understand Matt's needs more easily. Clearly Matt was happier and doing well in each of our households when there was peace and clarity between Jane and me.

My work and social life have been greatly influenced by child rearing. Like the great number of women and increasingly large number of men who combine careers with parenting on their own, I have often found the work doesn't support my parenting efforts. My bosses were indifferent to my home responsibilities and did little to meet my requests for flexible work hours. When Matt is with me I don't work at night or on weekends. To have the time flexibility I want and need, I became self-employed. Parenting responsibilities were not the only factor in this career decision, but they made me really think about what I wanted and valued.

When I was newly separated, social life meant Matt and me spending most of our time together. We explored museums, playgrounds, the zoo, and beaches, and we visited friends. Although I carefully separated my dating and my parenting, I often wanted adult company. Later, I would invite a friend to accompany us on our activities, and Matt usually felt OK about this—as long as I didn't pay too much attention to my friend.

The real problems started when I developed a serious relationship with Diane. Matt became intensely jealous. When Diane was visiting, he would demand my attention, act grumpy, interrupt and refuse to play alone. It's a wonder that my relationship with Diane survived that endless time of Matt's painful testing. He seemed to be making a last-ditch effort at keeping alive the hope that Jane and I would someday get back together. The night before Diane and I were to leave for our first vacation together, Matt cried his sorrow out, and this dream was over.

With hindsight, I more clearly understand why caring for Matt on my own has been so painful. Five years of experience has been a good education. When I first separated, I had been afraid so much of the time because what I was doing was new. There were no models, and there's a lot of unexplored territory between the family and the single father.

Parenting Matt means a lot more to me now than it did eight years ago. It means watching the clock so I can be on time to meet him after school, tracking down doctors, and taking him to the dentist, swimming class and the eye clinic. It means I have to remember his likes and dislikes when we shop for food and try to fit them in with my own sense of what's good to eat. I have to remember to get to teachers' conferences, to find time to talk with the parents of his friends, to force myself to read about child development and decide what's "normal." And as with any other parent, being a single father includes putting up with the Cub Scouts and the Little League, doing the laundry and housework, and making sure Matt washes his hands, takes a bath and cleans up his room. It means getting him to play in his room (not mine), finding out why he missed school, why he's mad at his friends or at his mother, or at me. And I have to listen to the endless details of movies and TV programs, stories, fights, and the current batch of eight-year-old jokes, and to learn how, tactfully, to stop his ceaseless chatter about all things interesting and not so interesting.

Sometimes when he is not with me I still miss Matt and worry about him, but the fear I used to have is gone. We have connections. Matt is eight and has his own world. He takes my hand only when he wants it. But my hand is still within reach. Shared custody works for us.

Harry F. Keshet
Cambridge, Mass.
January 1980

CHAPTER 1

Introduction to Fatherhood

This book focuses on two issues: the relationship between fathers and their children when the father is no longer legally married to the child's mother, and the effects of that relationship on the lifestyles and personal growth of these men and their children. The description we provide, the suggestions we offer, and the conclusions we make are based on very personal stories of one hundred and twenty-nine separated men. These men were selected on the basis of their continued attachment to their children as weekend fathers or full- and half-time single parents. They did not know each other. A few of them had no one to learn from, and had been unwilling to ask for help. Eventually, each man, by trial and error, worked out a pattern for his fathering.

In the book we have tried to put all these life stories together. We have discovered common problems and common solutions. We hope that these will not only help other fathers in the same situation, but also provide models and insights for all men, married and unmarried, as well as individuals and agencies who assist men in caring for their children.

Most of our respondents resided in an urban area. They were mainly young, white and middle class. They were likely to have a college background and to be engaged in professional, semiprofessional or white-collar work. The few respondents who worked as craftsmen or as skilled workers had more years of education than is generally the case for men in these groups.

The sample consisted of men who were available and willing to share their experiences. They constitute what we call a non-probability sample—that is, we cannot, at the present time, be certain how representative they are of the more than one million single fathers in the United States (Glick, 1975). We do know, however, that they represent a growing trend among separated fathers toward an increased involvement with their children.

Although each of the men might find himself in a somewhat different life situation with more or less money, different friends and helpers, different time commitments or priorities, the problems he faces are almost universal among the men who wish to maintain the bonds of fatherhood in the face of marital breakup. There are the conflicts between the spouses, the physical separation from the children, and, not infrequently, a legal system unsympathetic to the father's parental claims. Once a custody arrangement has been agreed upon, the demands of juggling work obligations and housekeeping tasks, and attending to the emotional welfare of the children, have been viewed quite similarly by all the fathers we interviewed.

We chose to interview men who had remained highly involved with their children after their marriages broke up, and who gave high priority to their fathering. This priority and the concern with the well-being of the children often served as guidelines for resolving the conflicts between the ex-spouses. Frequently, it became possible for the divorcing couple to reduce the conflict and begin to develop a more cooperative style, once the ex-wife became convinced of the sincerity of the father's intentions and his real commitment to the children's welfare. The fathers who were most clear about the importance of their continued relationship with the children were those who were already involved in child care before the separation. Although it is often assumed that children become pawns in the struggle between the divorcing parents, this was a rare occurance among our sample.

Social Science Neglects the Father

The sociological literature shows consistent bias in assumptions concerning appropriate parenting behavior. It presents "masculine" and "feminine" qualities as mutually exclusive and assumes that the behaviors beneficial to the development of children are those which belong under the label "feminine" and are thus not to be found in male parents, except as undesirable and deviant (Bell and Vogel, 1968). Benson (1968) reports having found widespread expressions of the belief that "the basic psychosomatic makeup of men provides them with little aptitude for child rearing" (p. 7). Expressions of similar attitudes can be found in the work of the majority of social theorists dealing with the family or parenting relationships. (Allen, 1965; Brenton, 1966; Fox and Steinman, 1974).

Nurturance has likewise been redefined as a female quality (Polatnick, 1973), with the result that men who are inclined to be nurturant suppress this quality for fear that their behavior will be seen as unmasculine. By defining behaviors which promote positive development in children as "maternal" (Bowlby, 1951; Parsons and Bales, 1955), the social scientists have given rise to a strongly adhered-to belief that the needs of children can only be met by the biological mother, or a female mother-substitute.

Many of the studies of so-called "maternal deprivation," showing the dire effect of "mother absence" for small children and, by implication, the importance of the mother-child bond, were based on observations of children who had neither mothers nor fathers present. In no instances were the adverse effects of maternal deprivation shown in children who had in fact been under the care of their fathers, or any other close and familiar adult. Kotelchuck (1973), in a critical review of both the maternal deprivation literature and the studies of mother-child interaction, points to the lack of comparative data on the role of the father. He concludes that the detrimental effects on child development can be more accurately ascribed to parental deprivation, or mis-parenting.

The literature on primates used as evidence for "natural"

parental behavior has suffered from the same assumptions (LeMasters, 1974; Harlow and Zimmerman, 1959; Harlow and Harlow, 1966). Here, as in the case of humans, the question of the role of the father is, for the most part, ignored. One exception, Mitchell (1969), reports that after close observation, one finds marked variations in actual primate behavior ranging from total child care involvement in the case of marmosets, where the fathers hold the babies whenever they are not being fed or groomed, through various intensities of involvement in the socialization of the growing monkey, up to total indifference. We may well expect the same range of behaviors, in the human species, depending on the individual characteristics and wishes of the human father. In general, the available theory and research direct attention to the mother and her expressive and nurturant functions, and to the father and his role as provider, authority figure, and coordinator between the family and the larger society (Mead, 1953; Parsons and Bales, 1955; Henry, 1963; Benson, 1968; Bigner, 1970). The characteristics which describe these two gender roles are seen as mutually exclusive. The research has rarely focused on actual parental behavior, and when it has, cases which did not conform to the expected behavior were labelled as deviant and assumed to be detrimental to all concerned.

Psychological literature similarly focuses both theory and research on the mother-child bond and neglects the role of the father in child development. Bowlby (1951), in his very influential work on early child development, limits the father's role to emotional and financial support to his spouse, so that she, in turn, can "devote herself unrestrictedly" to the care of the child. The equally influential book, *Beyond the Best Interests of the Child* (1973), which, for many years, has been the unchallenged reference for the legal profession, relies greatly on Bowlby's work and states unequivocally that when the father is no longer in harmony with the mother because of separation or divorce, he would best serve his child's interest by making himself scarce, so as not to interfere with the mother-child relationship. Dr. Benjamin Spock (1957), until the 1973 revision of his best-selling book on child care, took essentially the same position.

It is no wonder, then, that the major concern of married fathers who are on the brink of divorce is the threat to their parental relationship. We have found this to be almost universal among the men we interviewed, as well as in informal contacts, regardless of how involved the father was with his children before the breakup. The fathers who participated extensively in child care feared that the marital breakup would make it impossible for them to continue this level of involvement. Other men, who may have spent little time with their offspring except for a perfunctory "good-night," feared that the separation would deprive them of their children altogether and were brought up short by the realization of how little knowledge they had on which to build an independent relationship with them. For all men this was the time of questioning what their relationship to the children *ought* to be as well as what they would *like* it to be.

The Modern Family: Emotional Development of Men

The role of the male head of the family has been most clearly described by Parsons and Bales. These sociologists consider the father-husband's major task to be maintenance of the family as a social unit—that is, the father's work, his name, his reputation, and his status in life all represent the family to the larger society. The man's own sense of self-worth, in turn, depends on being able to maintain the family successfully. Since much of this success is a consequence of achievement in a job or a career, the male learns to conform to the expectations of the work world and to adjust his needs accordingly. This has been referred to as "instrumental" functioning: the male uses himself as an "instrument" to achieve the goal of social and economic status.

His wife-mother partner, on the other hand, takes on the responsibility for the emotional and physical well-being of the family members within the home. This extends to secondary relationships of friends, neighbors and acquaintances who are not related to the family through work. The husband may invite the boss to dinner, but the wife invites friends and relatives. To do her part, she must be sensitive to the needs of others and give priority to taking care of them. She attends to how they feel and what they need. And when relationships within the family are strained, she works hard to smooth things over. This is called "expressive" functioning.

This clear division of functions assumed in a conventional family presupposes a different set of values operating for men and women: his—achievement and financial success at any emotional or physical cost (as is often brought out in medical literature on stress associated with success); hers—emotional well-being at the cost of her own personal work achievement (as evidenced in the work and economic histories of women as a group). In such a conventional system, the father's rights and obligations within the family, such as the time he spends with his children, and the amount of services he expects from his wife, are based on a value system which originates outside the family and is not directly related to the needs of the family members. For example, in research on character training in families (Hess and Shipman, 1965; Blau and Duncan, 1967), it was found that the father's occupation determined his child-rearing practices. The fathers insisted on the kind of behaviors from their children which they saw as necessary in their own work.

Yet, within the often intensely emotional setting of the small family, many men find their work-world competence inappropriate. The child's temper tantrums, or the wife's emotional demands, leave them feeling helpless and inadequate. Veroff and Feld (1970) report that the high-achievement-motivated fathers are most likely to feel inadequate as fathers and inept with preschool children. Such men will hide behind the newspaper, or slump in front of the TV, or dash out with the boys whenever possible. They even return to their office at night, unneeded, to avoid being drawn into the emotional life of the family. It is not that these men do not love their families; it is just that having been highly trained for success in the work world, they have never been given the opportunity to develop an ease with intimacy. In close relationships they may have to draw on experience going back to their childhood, and thus their skill for dealing with close family members may not be developed—not a comfortable situation for a grown man. Many wives, sensing this, feel confused by what they see as a discrepancy in the behavior of their husbands. "I know he loves me," is a common cry, "but why can't he ever sit down and really talk to me?" For such men, sexuality may be the preferred means of "expressive" functioning which is otherwise unintegrated with the rest of their behavior. It tends to make them particularly limited in dealing expressively with children or other intimates with whom a sexual relationship is inappropriate.

This is not an outcome that Parson and Bales anticipate. They assume that by limiting the "instrumental" functioning to the work world and "expressive" functioning to the arena of family and intimate relationships, both will be able to develop to the fullest. They assume that the emotional and interpersonal aspects of each individual will be protected from possible exploitation outside the family.

In theory, then, the two parents, by behaving in these different ways and expressing different values and proprieties, are presenting to the child a totality of human behavior each within the appropriate sphere. In practice, however, the children see two adults of different gender moving away from each other in their increasing differences in areas of concern and life expectations.

Still, there are men who manage to develop nurturance and interpersonal skills and to integrate these into their masculinity. For the most part, such development is unnoticed and unappreciated except by those closest to them, and thus does not change the general expectations of male behavior.

Married Fathers and Their Children

In order to understand how men who are fathers view their role, and to be able to compare fathers outside of marriage to those who are living with their wives and children, we designed a questionnaire asking young married fathers to describe their parenting activities. These were distributed through day-care centers. The use of the day-care center provided us with a sample of families with young children, where both parents were employed and the father was more likely to be drawn into participation in child care.

A total of ninety-eight men returned our questionnaire. All but one had wives who worked at least part-time. Most respondents were highly educated and had either just begun to work or were completing professional training. Two-thirds worked full-time, and of those, two-thirds reported working many more hours than the conventional forty-hour week. A few of the men were students. The incomes varied widely, and only one-fourth of the men reported earning $20,000 or more.

We asked the men to describe an average day. The details of these fathers' daily lives with children were as follows: one-half reported waking up their child in the morning, and a small number also made breakfast and took their children to school. Most commonly, if a father did one of these tasks, he did all three. Conversely, picking up a child from school, making dinner or planning any activities with the children on *weekdays* was rarely reported. Fathers were also *not* the ones who took children to doctors or dentists or who took care of them when they were sick. The common child-parent activities of reading to the children at bedtime and playing indoor or outdoor games was reported by only a third of the men, but an equal number said they cooked dinner for their children once or twice a week and got up at night with them if necessary.

Although at first glance it may appear that the parenting of two working parents may be divided into morning and evening shifts, or weekend and weekday participation, in looking more closely at the active fathers we found this was not the case. Fathers who were the ones that woke up the children in the morning and got them breakfast were also most likely to be the same ones who put the children to bed at night and read them stories. In other words, the respondents did not divide into those fathers who took care of the children at night and those who did so in the morning, but rather into fathers who did much of the daily care and those who did very little. This was further corroborated by the lack of correlation between reported work hours of the father and the amount of child care: the fathers who worked more than full-time (some reporting over sixty hours a week) were just as likely to be the ones who got up with the child, made breakfast, and also took care of the child at bedtime, read to her or him and spent some time during the week playing with the child, as were those fathers working considerably fewer hours.

When asked about the important characteristics of a good father, "warmth" and "love" were mentioned by almost two-thirds of the fathers, and "sensitivity," "humor," and "honesty," as well as "patience and respect for the child" were each mentioned by half of the respondents. One-third of the fathers mentioned character training items such as "fairness," "firmness," and "guidance" or "discipline." There was no clear connection between the attitudes of the fathers on that question and their level of child care participation. When asked to rate themselves as fathers over half the respondents saw themselves as "above average." This self-rating, too, showed no relationship to degree of child-care participation.

The fathers who returned our questionnaire all thought of themselves as good parents, and this judgment might have influenced their willingness to tell us about themselves. Yet judging themselves as good parents had little to do with how much time they spent in parenting their child or whether or not they took part in daily child care tasks. It did not appear, therefore, as if there was a consistent standard of family behavior which could be used for self-evaluation.

Still curious as to sources of these men's concepts of fatherhood, we asked whether their own fathers had had the qualities they mentioned as important in a father. Fewer than one-third of the respondents remembered their own fathers as having these positive qualities, but the ones who did so were more likely to be the highly involved parents. This led us to speculate that though the ideas about how to be a good father may come from the current ideology and available child-rearing literature, the actual behavior of the men in the family is most likely to be a consequence of their own family experience.

When asked about major problems in the relationship with the child, the fathers most often mentioned their own shortcomings: "impatience," "expecting too much from the child," etc. Excessive demands on the part of the child were the second most commonly stated source of problems, and lack of time was cited by 20 percent of the fathers.

When asked to name the person who advises them on child rearing most of the fathers cited the spouse, "another relative" was second in frequency, and "a professional person" was cited by 20 percent of the fathers. One-fourth of the respondents said they get no advice from anyone.

For most men in our society, the degree to which they participate in caring for their children or performing household tasks is a consequence of an interaction between what they had learned as appropriate for a male in their own childhoods, and the expectations of their wives. The more his wife's expectations coincide with a man's own upbringing, the easier it will be for him to act on them. If he is, however, unable or unwilling to involve himself with the children, he has much social support for his resistence. Overtime work, community activities, sports, etc., are commonly used by some men to protect themselves from the demands of their families while at the same time sustaining the image of being "good," "hardworking," "ambitious" fathers.

Sometimes men are prevented from a more direct participation in the daily lives of their family by wives who feel threatened by such participation. For many women, parenting and care of the household have been the main areas of competence and control. Wives are often reluctant to share these activities with a man who has another professional life with its own set of rewards and satisfaction. "Don't mess up *my* kitchen" or "Here, let me do it," said to a man who is attempting to cook or change a baby, serves both to define an area of competence and to foreclose any possibility of either competition or cooperation. Many men may have found their well-meaning attempts at household participation subverted in this fashion, by women who had no other outlets for their own abilities and no other task where they could be needed and appreciated.

A man who participates only minimally in the family can be considered a "good" father as long as his behavior conforms to the expectations of his spouse. The frequency of his interaction with the children or the intensity of his relationship with them matters little, if he fulfills the expectations of being a provider or a protector or whatever is necessary to be an acceptable husband to the children's mother. Thus within the context of an intact marriage there is much flexibility in the role of the "good father." The married men interviewed rarely questioned their "fathering" unless some unusual family crisis pressed excessive demands on them, or unless their wives became critical of their family participation.

Within a stable family setting, then, there is no clear definition of the fathering role. After separation, however, when the role must be restructured independently, a clear understanding of the value and importance of the father-child relationship both for the father and the children becomes imperative.

The Significance of the Father in Child Development

As long as the "father's parental role is tied to the success and failure of the pair bond between himself and his wife" (Le Masters, 1974), which has been the prevailing view in America, it is difficult to determine the importance of the father-child relationship outside of the parents's marital status. Most discussions of the role of father are posed in terms of his function within the family or as a social representative of the family in the larger society. "The child grows towards the father" (Mead, 1965). The father, say the theorists, is the bearer of culture. This means that he represents the social adulthood; his contribution to the child is the reinforcement of the social self, the self of a unique individual growing towards maturity. We know from literature on child development (Lynn, 1974) that the father's task is to support the development of this autonomous self. Through his example as a functioning member of the outside world, through his behavior as an authority, through his approval and disapproval of his children's actions, the father facilitates the transformation of a dependent, vulnerable and typically egocentric new human being into a social person able to control his or her impulses and express his or her individuality.

It has been generally assumed that this function of the father can only be performed in the context of an intact family. In order to understand whether the traditional family structure is indeed a necessary aspect of the relationship between a father and child we must explain in greater detail the role of the father in the development of children.

Inasmuch as the mother is the organic parent, bonded to the child through the fulfillment of its basic physical needs, the father has the social assignment to lead the child out of its dependency into an appropriate expression of independence. In many primitive societies this assignment is very clear, especially for the male child. The father in many primitive groups actually takes the male child away from the mother at age seven or so and initiates him into the ways of men. In some cases the young son goes to live exclusively with men; in others, he undergoes rituals which separate him from his babyhood and identification with women, and serve to remind him of his adult destiny. Bettleheim in his book *Symbolic Wounds* (1954) gives an excellent discussion of the function of such rituals for males. The father must help his child to become whatever the particular society expects. Thus while the content of "mothering"—giving birth, feeding, cleaning, and providing other physical care—has been universal, the content of fathering has depended on the particular social situation and historical time. Thus social scientists have found it more difficult to describe or analyze this relationship, since they have not been able to observe universal behavior in the father-child relationship.

But the *dynamics* of the father-child relationship *are* universal. The father is the caring and involved adult who helps the child to separate from the mother, relieves the child of the guilt which might attend such a separation, and supports the fledgling autonomous self. In societies where women never venture beyond the domestic sphere, the father's role in their lives may be minimal, since the social expectations for adult females are very different from that for men. However, in a society like ours evolving towards an egalitarian structure, where the future is open to both men and women in nominally similar ways, the role of the father is important for the development of both boys and girls.

In other words, the image of the ideal father, and the age and gender of the child he most influences, may change with the changing social expectations for the adult futures of his children. The importance, however, of his participation is always true and increases when, as is the case in our society, autonomous adulthood is the desired outcome of socialization.

The foreboding, distant, post-Victorian father of the Freudian era was an appropriate socializer at a time when repression of spontaneous expression, especially of sexuality, was an expected characteristic of adulthood. Then, almost a century later, the athletic, friendly pal-father at the backyard barbecues of the nineteen-fifties became an ideal at a time when affable sociability seemed like a prerequisite for corporate success.

The developmental dynamics of the mother-child-father triad, described here, require a retranslation of the psychoanalytic concept of the Oedipal complex which still maintains a theoretical sway in this area of child development literature. Freud was struck by the myth of Oedipus who (having been raised as a stranger to his parents) kills his father and marries his mother, thus becoming king. When Oedipus discovers his true identity his triumph turns to guilt, remorse, and self-inflicted humiliation. Freud takes the myth to represent the universal emotions of the male child, who begins his life with an intense emotional attachment to the mother and with feelings of anger and rivalry towards the father, and because of his weak position vis-à-vis the father transforms the wish to get rid of him into a desire to become like him. Through this similarity the child hopes to eventually enjoy all the social privileges of the father. In this view the father must be both a strong opponent (to make it clear to the child that there is no advantage to the struggle) and a worthy model (so that the child may in fact benefit through the identification). It must be noted that while this model has been applied quite literally to the development of boys, its relevance for female children has been a source of confusion for psychologists.

We understand the Oedipus complex as a metaphor for transition from the dependency and infant love of the child through the agency of the father to the autonomy of adulthood. Ignoring the sexual connotation, we certainly agree that the mother-child bond is one of extreme intimacy and interdependence psychologically and physically. We agree with Erikson (1968) that early development of trust, and satisfaction of the child's dependency needs by the mother or other primary caretaker, is an important underpinning of later love relationships. As the child develops in the normal course of events, and becomes more independent and more assertive, the mother-child bond is weakened. A conflict arises between the assumed dependency and vulnerability of the child to which the mother responds, and the child's newly achieved competence. This can be seen in the many interactions of mothers with their small children or, in more extreme cases, in the explicit attempts of mothers to keep their children more dependent. Frequently, it is the father who encourages the child in his or her exploratory or risk-taking behaviors—"come on, jump; I'll catch you"—and the child's new competence can be expressed in the relationship with the male parent. Thus the development of an independent self—that is, the ability to deal with the world more independently—need not be seen as antagonistic to intimacy, even though it requires a greater distance from the mother, because it has a positive value in relating to another intimate, the father.

In our restatement of the Oedipal relationship, we view the confrontation with the father as an approach towards adulthood. This is not an antagonistic confrontation, but an increased intimacy based on independence and competence which makes the child "grow towards the father," as opposed to the dependency and vulnerability which is the basis for the mother-child bond.

When, like Oedipus, the child does not know the father—that is, no parental bond has been established whether the father is present or not—maturity is achieved through restructuring the relationship with the mother. The mother-child relationship continues to serve as a model for intimacy. Autonomy is viewed as destructive to intimacy and, conversely, intimacy as demanding a giving up of self. Males, especially, are likely to experience guilt over self-assertion and maintain a protective distance from a real or potential love object. Being an autonomous adult and being intimately connected with another are difficult to reconcile without the experience of a father's love to serve as a model.

When both parents are available to meet the different needs of the child, he or she should be able to express both vulnerability and a strong sense of self within a love relationship. Neither need be viewed as antagonistic to intimacy. This is surely one of the most important parental inputs, beside physical care. It is also a very difficult task for a mother to perform alone, no matter how aware and competent she may be as a parent. In encouraging the child to be independent, the mother is at the same time withdrawing, rejecting, or otherwise altering their previous relationship where the child's needs and wants had a great deal of power over her. She is freeing herself in the process, and the time and energy she has given to the child can now be used in her own pursuits. Thus, the most loving attempt at independence training by a mother has in it the elements of creating boundaries, which although necessary, separate the mother and the child in ways they both recognize.

It is not uncommon that a child will behave quite differently in the mother's absence. For example, a small child who usually insists on the mother's assistance in getting dressed, or putting away toys, or preparing a snack, may do these tasks quite competently and independently when she's not there. When she is present again, however the child may redouble his or her insistence on the mother's help.

When these behaviors occur in children who are spending time with separated parents, they are often misinterpreted. The father, when the children are with him, will be quite pleased with what he views as his effectiveness in demanding independence and will be concerned that the mother is "babying" or spoiling the youngster, particularly if the child in question is male. The mother, in turn, views the child's increased demands upon her when he or she is back at her home as a sign that the father has not provided enough care or that the visit has been stressful. What both parents fail to understand is that they are observing, in more encapsulated and intensified form, behavior which is normally incorporated into the pattern of family life.

What has really happened is that the time with the father has provided the child with an opportunity to try out some newly acquired skills and autonomy drives, counting on the approval and increased interest from the father. This new behavior is seen by the child as a way of maximizing the relationship with the father. Since both the child's autonomy and the closeness to the father threaten the mother-child bond, especially when the parents are not together, the child's next move is to seek reassurance about that bond: "Now that I can tie my own shoelaces and dress myself to go out with Dad, do I still have the power to make Mom take care of me?" Hence the bout of dependency when the mother appears.

Consider this scene—a snapshot captured in many family albums: A smiling young woman is releasing a tottering toddler from her arms, and the child takes a few trial steps into the outstretched arms of the young man facing her. This captures the essence of the relationships. The mother stays back ready to support the toddler should he or she fall back; the father waits ahead ready to reward the child for the courage and skill of these first steps. In the same way as the toddler will not take his or her first, scary, steps towards a total stranger, or even a casual acquaintance, so the older child will not "grow towards the father" unless that father already represents a desirable, trusted, and loved presence in the child's life. It matters little if he lives with the child's mother, if he is the economic provider or the stern disciplinarian, or if he fits any of the other conventional images of fatherhood. What matters is that he should be available to his child and open to the growing relationship between them. He should love his child and express that love in attention, approval, and continuous interest. This, as we will see, can be, and has been, arranged in or out of a marriage.

We do not mean to imply that these behaviors are rigidly parcelled out between the parents. The mother does eventually say: "You're old enough to walk by yourself now; I'm not going to carry you," and in doing so she is being both supportive to the child's new growing self and rejecting of his or her dependency. She will not be too consistent; she will again accede to these needs when they arise, as when the child is tired, the road is difficult, etc; she will remain ready to understand and accept the falling back, the regression. Eventually the mother-child relationship will evolve slowly out of needs and demands into one in which the mother is less and less needed, and her offers of help may be indeed rejected as the children growing into adolescence more and more assert their autonomy.

The father, too, has had experience meeting the needs of the children, and they would not be able to take risks with their new-found freedom unless they could count on his protection. Through early child-care feeding, bathing, and getting up at night with the child, the father is introduced as a person to be trusted and relied upon, and some of the natural bonds existing between a child and the mother are transferred to the father. Seen from the father's point of view, this kind of early child care allows the father to see his children at their most needful and vulnerable time, making it appropriate for him to respond with concern and affection. This bond of affection must be the background for any more conventional fatherly function of modeling and discipline, if the child is to be led into adult modes of behavior with love and trust.

Since men tend to defer to their wives in the area of early child care, it is important that they have the opportunity to spend time alone with their children. When the mother is present the bonding is less likely to occur, especially since men look to women for nurturant activities so important in the interaction. The father whose only time alone with the children is spent at the playground is less likely to create the kind of emotional bond with his child that will give credence and power to his later interaction with the maturing offspring.

This formulation of the importance of the father-child relationship has made us proponents of co-parenting as an ideal both for intact marriages and postdivorce arrangements. It is necessary that the father share in the everyday activities of the child and attend to the mundane tasks of child care. Whether the time between the parents is actually shared equally is a matter of convenience and practicality, but it is not necessary. Continuing as a supportive parent after separation does open the father to additional obligations, whether it is a matter of providing financial and emotional support for the child's mother, interceding with the teacher or making time for child-oriented activities. A father who takes real pleasure in his child's development is very likely to be willing to do whatever is necessary to enhance the context for that development by cooperating with the other adults involved in the child's life. He learns to negotiate for his continued involvement, and to deal with his ex-wife in ways that are most likely to protect his relationship to his children.

Traditional Views of Men and Child Care

When we think of child care we automatically think of women. Almost any female who is of pleasant disposition and in good health is seen as a suitable potential caretaker for children, either her own or someone else's. But the suitability of men for child care, not even of any one man in particular, is often questioned. While motherhood has been studied, written about and lectured on from the point of view of everyone concerned, from mothers and children to social scientists and philosophers, fatherhood until quite recently (Lynn, 1974; Atkin and Rubin, 1977; Levine, 1977) has been one of the least described relationships. Men's own attitudes toward the fathering role have for the most part never been reported.

The specific role of father, describing the kind of family participation beneficial to children rather than the deficits of "father absence" has been a neglected area of research in the social sciences. Only one major study of American families in the past twenty years used direct interviews with fathers to investigate the parental roles (Seeley, 1956). More frequently the data was gathered through interviews with wives and children (Miller and Swanson, 1958) or through analysis of literary works or popular media (Benson, 1968).

Fathering can take many different forms. When we look at different cultures we find two universal aspects of fathering: one is the assignment of a child to an adult male relative, not necessarily its biological genitor (in some societies the mother's brother assumes the social fatherhood); and a close relationship which develops between the child and its "acting" father through daily contact. It is the task of the father to protect the child and to slowly introduce him (less often her) to the adult world. In our own culture fathers are defined as such primarily because of their biological bond and marriage to the child's mother. The direct relationship with the child is not a necessary feature of the role; thus it is possible to have loving and involved fathers as well as "distant fathers, disinterested fathers, absentee fathers, demanding fathers, and fathers who without lifting a hand to help a child may be exigent and relentless in their demands" (Mead, 1965).

In general, the fathering bond is more social than biological and depends more on the values and expectations of the given culture than on emotional bonding between child and parent. Not many cultures encourage men's participation in the birth process, although this has been a recent trend in our own society. A few societies interpret pregnancy as a joint activity, and in these, fathers may be expected to experience sympathetic physical symptoms. Sometimes special rituals may be designed to allow the father to welcome the child at the moment of birth. It is usually the case in any culture that fathers feel more comfortable with their children as the children grow older. "From the moment of birth the child grows towards the father," says Mead. The more active the father's participation in the care of the infant the stronger the bond between them, yet our own culture does little to support the involvement of a man with his small children.

Most recently, the change in expectations about the role and behavior of women has turned the trend in the direction of increased participation by men in all spheres of domestic activities, including the care of children. "Parenting has become a desirable male role for many, and fathers are accepting major parenting responsibility within the two-parent family context and the single-parent context" (Roland, 1975).

Historical Roots of Parental Roles

We are by no means implying that men have not in the past participated in child care. They have often been the sole parents in charge, either because they had so desired or because circumstances demanded it. It is important, however, to remember that when they did take care of children, they viewed themselves, and were seen by others, as "substitute mothers." The "poor widower" with small children, the wronged husband whose wife had deserted him, or the divorced man who had fought for the custody of the children because of the presumed unsuitability of their mother—all these men were seen as being in great need of female assistance and as objects of pity. Thus the experience of child care rarely became an accepted part of the normal life histories of men.

To place the issue of child care in an even more general context we must consider the evolution through history of the place of children in the family. We commonly find the phrase "traditional family" or "traditional family roles" used to describe a family in which the wife stays home to take care of the children while the husband supports the family with his labor. Yet how recent is this "tradition?" In the past, a family group had been a production unit as well. It consisted of adults, children and servants. Many people lived and worked under the same roof, in crowded situations, well into the mid-eighteenth century. Those who were too poor to afford servants were often too poor to keep their children as well. In wealthier households, the number of servants nearly always exceeded the number of children. Thus, looking at old paintings or reading old accounts of daily life, we see children in the company of servants often not much older than themselves, or else fending for themselves in groups of peers, their behavior differing little from those of the adults around them.

Children were passed on to wet nurses, sent away as apprentices, child brides, small servants, or little scholars. Although the care of infants and toddlers fell to females, these were not necessarily mothers themselves, and often they were not even adult women. Men and women were equally responsible for the economy of the family (Oakley, 1974). Phillippe Ariès in *Centuries of Childhood* (1962) wonderfully describes the growing awareness of childhood as a particular stage of life requiring specific attention and instruction.

The major difference between the medieval and the seventeenth-century family, says Ariès, is the return of the children to the home. Previously they had been entrusted to the care of strangers, either out of necessity or because of custom. The home they returned to, however, was not like the modern family. It was filled with kin and workers, and the children continued to be under the direct care of adults other than their parents, even though now under the same roof and the same general management of the parent-master couple. This evolution from the medieval family through the succeeding centuries and on to the modern family was limited for a long time to the nobles, the middle class and the richer artisans and laborers. A large part of the population, the poorest section, were still living like the medieval families, with children separated from their parents.

Ariès finds the concept of the family unchanged from the eighteenth century to the present. What has changed, he says, is the extension of family life throughout all the strata of society "to such an extent that people have forgotten its aristocratic and middle class origins." With the disappearance of the cousins, grandfathers, younger uncles, resident tutors and friendly laborers from the home and the everyday experience of the child, only the parents are left. It seemed no longer appropriate for the father to remain a distant authority, and he now became the playmate and teacher as well. We can easily see how the increased demands on the parents, on the small isolated nuclear family, both intensified and confused the parental relationship.

One might argue, however, that the concept of the family has not only changed over the centuries, but that it is in fact continually in flux. The medieval and postmedieval household, as Ariès describes it, is a center of economic activity. The *paterfamilias* heads the family clan as well as the business enterprise. The status of children is shared by the servants and the workers.

When the family unit ceases to be the work unit as well, the bearing and raising of children emerges as the next clearest definition of familial ties. Regardless of the type of economic or social structure, we find that a universal priority is given to procreation. In some societies marriage may be broken when one partner is infertile or sterile. In others, a family unit will not be formed until a child is born, or at least expected. In still others, extramarital sex is condoned as long as the children are accepted as belonging to an intact family. The often-voiced concern of the modern couple to maintain their marriage "for the sake of the children" attests to the primacy of the child care for the family unity.

This attitude first began to change in the thirties with the reality and the ideal of decreased family size. The reasons for becoming a family, or at least for marriage—and the distinction between the two has not usually been kept clear—began to focus on intimacy between adults. The interest shifted to the parental couple and to an increasing introspection into emotional and sexual lives of adults. This shift has heralded the institution of the "companionate" marriage—one where the two adults satisfy each other's emotional needs. It has also helped to obscure the role of children in the family. The nineteenth-century tracts extolling the virtues of parenthood and the blessedness of fertility has given way to a view of children as an economic and psychological barrier to perfect adult intimacy. To put it bluntly, it has become legitimate to wonder whether children were worth the trouble and to make deliberate decisions for or against parenthood. Although women continue to be considered, often against their protestations, as being "naturally" destined for motherhood, the question about the advantage of parenthood for men has not been so easy to answer now that the children are no longer needed to help on the farm, expected to support parents in their old age, or bring honor to the family name.

It is one of the purposes of this study to illuminate this question. We found men who made many sacrifices in terms of their own comfort or achievement in order to spend time with their children. This was often neither expected of them nor encouraged, even by their own immediate family. Why did they do it? What bound them to their children, and how did they benefit by that relationship?

Once such questions may have seemed peculiar, or likely to be answered in moral terms. But today, we find ourselves at a time of conflicting cultural expectations, especially when it comes to the issue of family responsibility. On one hand, most of us still share the images of the "ideal" or "traditional" family—two parents, a private residence, outsiders helping only occasionally or in an emergency. Each adult does his or her assigned part, and the children are obedient and grateful but leave home upon maturity as a sign that their parents have done their "job" well. On the other hand, there is confusion as to what can be expected of the children. Should they support their parents in old age, care for them in case of illness? What do the children expect of the parents beyond childhood care? Once people who did not have children were viewed as selfish. Now, sometimes, bringing children into the world is viewed as selfish. The current emphasis on individual fulfillment and self-actualization often leaves parents confused about the values related to their parenting obligations.

CHAPTER 2

On Becoming a Father: Men's Images of Marriage and Family

Four Case Studies

We chose to present the life histories of four men who were willing to speak freely about the events of their marriages and childhoods, and whose backgrounds and attitudes differed enough to provide a range of values and experiences. What they have in common is coming to full adult responsibility in the seventies, when the pervasive value of permissiveness encouraged and facilitated important life changes. They reminisced as far back as their childhood for the sources of their understandings about the family. Here we have the stories of four men whose adolescence was full of dreams of future success, whose wives were attractive and intelligent (a seemingly necessary accessory to their expected achievements), and whose marriages, so hopefully entered into, nevertheless ended in divorce.

The men were the originators, perpetrators and sometimes victims of the sexual revolution, the increased geographical mobility, and the women's movement. They have experienced a great deal of personal change and disruption which they may eventually come to see as beneficial. They were forced to examine their lives, to grow, and to make decisions. The final judgment about the meaning of these events rests with the social historians of their children's generation.

The men we interviewed were born in the late thirties or early forties. Their lives tailed the Depression years, still very real for their parents, although they themselves grew up in relative comfort. From our own study, as well as from other data and literature, it seems that this generation has experienced a pervasive sense of emotional distance from their parents. Each of the men was motivated by a desire to have a life different from that of his parents. There were few direct models for the kind of life these men hoped to lead, only untried fantasies.

We will let Larry, Don, Bill and Rob tell the story in their own words; we have changed it only minimally to protect their identities. From these stories we can learn much about how men grow up in our culture.

Adolescent Fantasies

Larry, an intense young man who shifts between a desire for total freedom and a clearly lived-out need to be connected to other people and ideological lifestyles, perhaps best typifies the times. He has been separated from his wife, Rachel, for the last two years and has a six-year-old daughter, Vita. Larry and Rachel are still working out ways to share raising their daughter. They disagree on many child-rearing issues and often Larry wishes he had Vita all to himself, but for most of the time they have worked out some kind of a half-time schedule.

We asked Larry to tell us about himself, going as far back in his life as he felt was relevant in thinking about his marriage.

I guess I'd have to go back to high school. I was a loner and an intellectual snob. I was sure I'd never marry. My life with my parents was not very happy; I was miserable, in fact. I thought having a family would be getting trapped in another unhappy scene.

From sixteen on I was extremely independent, though I still lived at home. They were really OK to me then, very liberal; they respected my rights. There was still an awful tension between us but I was no longer at their mercy the way I felt when I was a little child.

I wanted to quit high school and go off and be a beachcomber and write. I guess everyone has these fantasies. But I went on to the university, hoping to find my place in life there. It did not happen. It was not a place where they recognized anyone's talents or abilities. The only recognition I could get was by working my ass off studying and I wasn't interested in most of what was being taught . . . So after three months I quit.

I was going to be a poet, a motorcyclist, and a lover. Sort of a combination of Brando, Dean and Dylan Thomas. The perfect image for me at that time. I was into drinking, and when I could get my hands on it, grass. Also, well, I am not sure whether I should say women, or girls. I did not think I was ever going to stop being foot-loose and fancy free. There was a spiritual side to me too. I thought of becoming a bramachari, a single person who leads the spiritual life—no responsibilities, no material needs; it was a way of being religious. Later on, it was that part of me that led into wanting to be married.

What did you do after you quit school?

I hitched around the States. Every single one of my middle-class contemporaries was at college. It was outrageous when I quit. By the summer I came back and worked for my father. In the fall I went back to college. I stayed for three years till I was twenty. I got more and more conflicted about it. I was in terrible shape. I fell into the clutches of a Freudian analyst who did nothing for me. It's awful how people fool themselves into thinking that they are helping someone.

What about relationships with women?

When I was between sixteen and seventeen I had my first real love. That's all we did; now I can't imagine making love as many times and as often as we did. Stupendous!!! I feel like a middle-aged man looking at myself now. Then she got pregnant. At first we talked like we were going to get married. I would be an English professor, and we'd lead this very proper life. I went along with it, but I knew it wasn't me. Finally we had to deal with the pregnancy for real. We got frantic. She said, "How about marriage?" and my answer was 100 percent no. It was a terrible time.

In the third year of college, I split again. My therapist went out of town on a vacation. He had been doping me pretty heavily with tranquilizers. I took off and went to the coast to see if I could get a job on a ship. I wanted to go to the South Sea Islands. By this time I was into the spiritual stuff again. I did Yoga and went to ashram almost every weekend. I could not get a job on a ship although I tried very hard. So I went to an ashram for six months and studied meditation.

Then I went to San Francisco—that was 1967. What a great time to be there! Before the mass media built it up.

In San Francisco I became involved in a community of people who were into counterculture Yoga and spirituality. I was living with friends who were married and had a child. It looked good. I liked what was happening for them, and I thought I wanted the same for me.

Our next interviewee, Don, was one of the oldest men in our sample. At the time of the interview he had been separated for three years. He married at the age of twenty-nine and had three children from the marriage whose ages were twelve, ten, and six. Don saw them every other weekend.

Don's childhood and adolescence occurred at an earlier time than Larry's, and were a great deal more conventional. In fact, Don was definitely not the adventurous type, nor would his family have tolerated an adventurous adolescence.

As a boy I had a lot of problems. I was not athletic and got picked on a lot. I spent a lot of time fantasizing about sports and later about sex.

When we played ball on the street I was always the last one chosen. I read a lot; had two or three friends who were like me and we would play Monopoly or read comic books, do quieter stuff than most of the other kids.

I had a lot of hassles with my mother. Once I wouldn't do something and she started to hit me with a ladle. I ran out and decided to run away. That was at noon. At evening I decided to go home. She had the whole neighborhood looking for me, and everyone was tearful and sorry.

That felt good. It was sort of a back-ass way of asserting myself. I'd fight with my mother sometimes, but neither one of us ever won. I felt as if she never listened to anything I said.

My mother was never emotionally giving, and all I remember of my father is sitting quietly around the house reading the newspaper. Sometimes he washed the dishes or helped my mother with house-work. He was timid and undemonstrative. Occasionally he took me places but never exciting ones.

I have one sister, eight years younger than me. There was very little relationship between us—eight years is a big gap.

Last year I went to see my parents with the kids, and after four days I said to my father, "Dad, you've hardly talked to the kids; you don't pay much attention to them," and he said, "Yes, that's the way I've always been; that's the way my father was." Indeed, I remember my father's father. When we visited him he would say, "Hello, Don" and that might be the only words he'd say for three hours.

I always felt my father was just there to do what my mother told him to do. I never remember him having a friend of his own. I remember a few times when he would be a little demonstrative and she would push him away. I still find it hard to believe that they ever made love.

I never shared anything emotional with my father, only general things; it seemed useless, he would not understand. Later when I got out of college with an engineering degree and wanted to go into social work, he said, "I'd rather see you dead than a social worker." That seemed to be so out of character for him that it frightened me. When I was getting married, at the age of twenty-nine, he said, "I guess it's no use telling you about sex, you must know by now." He didn't even use the word *sex*.

I felt as if I had nobody to learn from; as a model my father just was not there. I got a sense of what a boy or a man is from other kids, reading, all the stereotypes. But the area of emotions was completely missing. I don't even remember ever hearing an adult man talking about emotions until my divorce. I never showed my feelings, just sat on them. I covered it all up with activity. As a college student I was into everything—a big man on campus. There was a lot of interesting people and I was outwardly very successful . . . and feeling shitty. There is still that dichotomy in my life. I never opened up the emotional side of myself, didn't really understand it, and didn't want to expose my weaknesses.

Don is quite typical of many of the men we interviewed in seeing his family as distancing and unemotional. Investigations of relationships between fathers and sons often disclosed the prevalent unavailability of the father to his children, particularly in urban families. He is unavailable either because he is away at work for a great portion of the child's waking time, absorbed in a newspaper or TV when he is home, "resting," or unavailable emotionally even when he is doing something with his children. As one man put it, "My father used to do carpentry with me, but when I hurt my finger, he sort of disappeared and my mother would rush over to take care of me."

What a boy tends to learn is that to be emotionally unavailable is one of the masculine behaviors. And as he is frequently not even aware that the lack of warmth on the part of the father hurts other members of the family, himself included, he often learns to accept disregarding the needs and feelings of others as something that a man does when necessary.

Even as the son has difficulty learning how to be different from the father, he harbors a great deal of resentment. In a study of college seniors (Komarovsky, 1976), lack of paternal warmth headed the list of expressed dissatisfaction within the family. Fathers were characterized as lacking in warmth, understanding, and acceptance. And although sons declared themselves closer in outlook to their father than to their mother, one half of the men described ties with their father as "neutral" and "strained." This combination of seeing themselves not unlike the father and yet resenting the father's behavior makes many men insecure about their own family membership, and that much more vulnerable to feelings of guilt and inadequacy when their marriage breaks up.

The confusion about what is good male behavior makes a boy susceptible to the influence of his male peers. As he moves out of the world of the family, he is careful to conform to the stereotypes of masculinity prevalent among the group he goes around with. Later, it is the woman he cares about who will serve as the main judge and evaluator of whether or not he is an adequate male. In the study mentioned above, Komarovsky found that a female friend was the most likely person to whom male college seniors confided, and that the frequency of such confidences went up when the son reported an unsatisfactory relationship with the father.

While both Larry and Don seemed to be escaping from a family where emotionality did not support communication, our next respondents came from families where few real feelings were expressed. Rob was a man whose separation from his father was caused by death.

I'd been very sheltered, suburban, all WASP. I really did not have much sense of what the world was like. Then I had a series of disillusionments, starting with the death of my father when I was 16 and going on to lose my faith and religion which I had as a child. About the time I went to college I became increasingly cynical about things I had believed in while growing up. I was learning a whole lot from other people with different backgrounds and from my teachers and my classes.

I associated being married with a humdrum, suburban, blasé existence. It was a trap. I think I did expect to be married sometime. But the first time I remember thinking about it was when I did get married. I knew people in college who had gotten married, or even left college to get married; I thought they were crazy. It was great to be on my own, drinking beer, staying up late, doing lots of things my mother never let me do. Getting married seemed like growing old before your time.

I remember one time talking to a guy who I worked with one summer. He was married and we started discussing sex. He showed me pictures of his wife, who was very attractive. Somehow it came out that they didn't have sex every time they went to bed together. I was mystified that with a wife as pretty as that, he would not want to screw every chance he got. My idea of marriage became associated with getting bored with sex.

Images of Husbanding

Not unlike Rob, Bill, who separated from his wife when his daughter was a year and a half, also had little notion of what real family life was like. With the III appended to his name he was constantly told he had come from a lineage of responsible citizens in his community and must live up to that image. But Bill felt his grandfather was the last of the family who seemed truly to deserve this reputation. Bill's own father, a model citizen in the town, went swimming one day at an ocean beach and when his things were later found abandoned on the beach he was presumed to have drowned. His family mourned him and his funeral was attended by many. Four years later he reappeared. He had left for Europe, unable to carry the burden of his family life. There, he had married again, and when he returned—out of guilt or curiosity—he had already fathered one more child by another wife. Perhaps by that time the new life and the old life had blurred. His return caused distress to his family that was perhaps greater than his faked death. It took many years for Bill to forgive his father. "I guess it was the only way out he had. I guess I have resources open to me that he never had." Nevertheless, Bill grew up concerned about responsibility, reserved to the point of being withdrawn, and unsure of himself in relationships.

It happened that the men interviewed did not feel close to their families. We do not know how representative that is of men who are involved in a divorce. We do know that for many men their determination to stay in close contact with their children, and, indeed, what they did with their children even while they were married, seems to be influenced by the desire *not to duplicate* the kind of fathering that they had received. So they have tried hard to be present, to be caring, and to be available to their children; yet the images of manhood available to them and the behavior they have known to be expected of men has not supported their desire to be nurturant and family oriented.

Even in the most stable of families boys are rarely expected or encouraged to develop emotional skills, and these skills are rarely taught at home or in school. If the father himself is understanding and communicative, then the model is there. And it is a very important model. Boys who have such fathers never fail to mention how important that was to their growing years. But as we see in the Komarovsky study, such fathers are not common. Most male children learn about themselves from sources outside the family—that is the place where their thinking and doing is rewarded. Independence and achievement, the two most encouraged and expected male behaviors, happen in the context of a gradual separation from the family. When a boy reaches adulthood and thinks about being intimate with a woman, he attempts to translate what he has learned as important to being a man to the conduct of an intimate love affair. But the qualities needed to develop interpersonal relationships and to satisfy the need for closeness differ from those leading to achievement and independence. In fact, he often finds a great conflict between what he has learned is important to him as a male and what seems to be required of him for the happiness of his life with another. For example, in order to maintain the *independence* he is proud of, he feels he must maintain a degree of distance from the loved one. To be very close may be interpreted as abandoning independence.

Achievement, on the other hand, may be viewed in terms of competition and rewards. For the men socialized for work, achieving in the area of relationships with women requires the sense of creating rewards, an experience of winning and of superior performance.

When our respondents described their notions of being husbands and fathers, we saw very clearly that emphasis on competence, self-sufficiency, the image of the strong silent male. Although a wife is expected to be sensitive to her husband's needs, to understand him, and to care for him, few men are prepared to explain their emotional needs or to admit that they may be in need. Men who do not feel free to express their feelings or emotions may behave as if emotions did not exist. They pay little attention to their own emotional needs or to those of others. It often takes the extreme discomfort of marital breakup to break open the dammed-up feelings and refuse to hide them any longer.

It is this ability on the part of men to ignore or deny the emotional side of their relationships that accounts for so many stories of married men who seemed not to know that their marriage had gone wrong until they were so informed by their wives. These men often expressed shock and dismay. It seems as if their wives have gone "crazy." One wonders, on hearing such stories, how it is possible to live closely with a mate and yet remain seemingly so unaware of the true nature of the changing relationship.

Bill said:

I tried to be responsible financially, and to take care of whatever had to be done. When a problem came up I thought it was up to me to solve it. It was very easy for me to contain my anger; I had in my blood five generations of nice people who never said a word in anger. And I was not the kind of person who could talk about himself. Hell! I didn't know enough about myself to know what to talk about. I would have liked to be open with people, but it seems like then people just were not that intimate. We didn't know how to talk to each other. When you don't have much self-knowledge, you're not in a position to be open to anyone.

Rob said:

I thought of a husband as being a very competent, together person, emotionally very self-sufficient, not making emotional demands on the wife. I would be good in dealing with the outside world: insurance, fixing up a house, etc. I expected my wife to be very sensitive of where I was emotionally without my having to tell her. She was to receive my messages without my ever sending them, and to accommodate herself to them. My thinking was very traditional; I expected that I would be the primary wage earner while my wife stayed at home with the kids. I was going to be a loving father and gentle with the kids, but that would be confined to evenings and weekends. When we were older, we would work around the house or something, that's what I experienced in my house. I assumed I would be the stricter parent and my wife would be more permissive.

Larry responded:

Well, I had this idea that I would marry, live in the country, do crafts, and maybe I'd be a spiritual leader. I thought I'd be very gentle, kind and caring; that was my husband image. My wife would be spiritual too, very dedicated to the children, involved in tending the house, the garden, and very supportive of me. I imagined my wife would have beautiful long hair and a full body!

And Don said:

I had very little feeling for men-women relationships growing up. My father was a very contained, quiet guy. He always seemed warm, but it was hard to make a connection with him. My mother was agressive and domineering. They seemed very separate. Marriage was an institutional thing that I accepted as something I had to do. As I went through my twenties I thought about marriage, and each time I got close, I pulled away. I even got engaged once and broke the engagement. I was engaged to a very emotional, outgoing woman, and at that point emotional women just scared the shit out of me.

The conventional images of the competent, decisive husband came into conflict with the actual stories of the early marriage. The men we interviewed rarely married the women they had described in their imagination; they rarely felt that the marriage represented a controlled and thought-out decision, and rarely experienced themselves as the self-assured active males they respected.

Getting Married

Larry, whose fantasies were of a soulmate and a spiritual cohort with long hair and a full body, described how he met his wife while he was living in a religious commune:

One day a girl they knew came for the weekend. She got sick and ended up staying in the house for a long time. She stayed in a bed next to mine in a tiny, tiny room. I got to like her and we just sort of stayed together.

As a spiritual seeker I was looking for a soulmate in a woman. I was not sure that Rachel was it, but we started to travel around together. We never stayed any place longer than six weeks. I still felt I was foot-loose and would live an unconventional life. After nine months we started to live together.

And was Rachel all those things you had wanted in a wife?

No, I guess not. There were, in fact, lots of things I did not like about her. I broke off the relationship a week before I asked her to marry me.

Then we saw each other again and it was kind of nice so I thought, Oh, what the hell! We got married when I was twenty-two.

We had a great wedding. It was in my home town, and eleven of our friends came.

We moved to Oregon and got a place in the country with a garden. I worked at becoming a jewelry maker, but Rachel wanted to go to the university, and I was very against that. The place was great; we had lots of guests, lots of celebrations, but we were not at all happy with each other.

There is much to suggest in the interviews that the early days of the marriage is often a time of inattention. That is, each partner is happy assuming that their common life plans are being realized, while in fact, more often, each is going their own way, unaware of the distance they are creating.

Rob's images of the emotionally self-sufficient husband and the super-sensitive wife were also belied by the actuality of his marriage to Beth.

I guess I was timid, though I did not consciously think of myself as timid. I didn't know myself very well. Now, I think I was testing limits and I was both exhilarated and scared by it. I didn't know what was going to happen to me. I met Beth when we were both students at the university. She had just enrolled and I was a senior, but she seemed much more sophisticated politically than me. And politics was the big thing on campus in those days. She was from an activist family and I was just a dull Republican. Her background and politics meant all sorts of forbidden fruit to me—sexually as well as politically. I stereotyped her a lot, assumed she was both sexually and politically liberated. She also impressed me as a very vivacious, outgoing, warm, and friendly person. I saw myself as more conservative and timid and thought that she would draw me out.

I sort of backed into marriage without thinking about what it was. I just thought of it as a paper thing I was doing to satisfy my parents. We were both still in school and our parents were concerned how we would support ourselves. So we decided not to have kids for a while, but we did assume that eventually we would be parents.

What were those early married days like? (Rob)

We shared the cooking and the housekeeping, but she took the initiative. I didn't do it until she mentioned that it had to be done. I think for a long time she cooked and I did the dishes. I always paid the bills. I think when we first lived together before we were married we shared doing the laundry, but after we bought a washer Beth did it by herself. We started to live together in the fall of the year I graduated and started in graduate school; we got married the next summer, nine months later.

For Bill it meant a decision to move to the country, where he was working as a teacher and building his own house, while Lisa, his wife, was learning to be a weaver and planning a studio of her own.

We liked each other and had a pretty decent, loving relationship. But we were not too open with each other. If you don't have much self-knowledge then you're not in a position to be open to someone. We talked as much as we could, but we were afraid.

Bill was not sure what they were afraid of—perhaps of finding out that their lives were not what they thought them to be. Sex was one of those things they did not talk about.

When we were splitting up (five years later) is when we finally talked about fucking. Wow, what a relief. Someone I'd slept with for five, six, seven years and we never talked about it. We knew we did not have a very good thing, but then again, we thought it was better than most.

Larry was much more understanding of his own relationship.

What were those early married years like?
She cooked, canned, and froze food, but she was also going to school and I hated that, and she was upset that I hated it. She did most of the housework too; she cleaned with my assistance, she did the laundry and the dishes; when I did them it was as a favor to her. First, we lived on the money from our wedding, which was fine with me, but not with her. So she got a job as a part-time bookkeeper for a while. After a few months my jewelry started to sell and I could support us with that. I worked all the time, all day, but I could pay all our bills.

But there was a lot of tension between us. Rachel did not like being a farm wife, I did not like her going to school. After we'd been married about six or seven months she stayed out all night and slept with someone. That made things very bad between us; she wasn't liking what I wanted her to be and I was not letting her be who she really was.

We decided maybe we should go some place else, so first we went to the West Coast to California and then to New Mexico. I guess it was a way to get her to quit school.

While in California we met some friends who were deciding to go to Mexico, so we decided to go with them. By June 1969 we were in Mexico. It was difficult to get used to a new place, a new language and a different climate. I became a jewelry worker again, although I thought I'd do something else. We both did crafts in Taos and made a living with it. Although I still wanted to be spiritual, it was a different way of being spiritual than was true at the Ashram. People there followed a strict code of laws. We always bent that code; it was hard to even talk about it there. At first I looked for a spiritual teacher, but then I stopped expecting to find one and was just satisfied to be with my friends.

Our goal was to find a place to live. We decided to settle in a very small town and traveled around to find one. We finally found a village we liked, and after we settled there it seemed like a good place to have a child. And Vita was born there.

I earned my living teaching school. I planted the most exquisite garden for pleasure, and a fruit orchard. We had dozens and dozens of different varieties of shrubs and trees. I also studied the Scripture every day with a friend. I was not very involved with the baby.

It was hard on Rachel. I was very autocratic and she could not deal with a lot of things, but also could not talk about them. She really wanted to go back to school and I was still very opposed to that. All the other women in our group of friends were completely involved with their families, and their houses. That to me was the appropriate counterpart in a woman to what I was doing and wanted to do. Rachel felt trapped, cooped up and dissatisfied. I was in seventh heaven. I loved my work; I had friends nearby. It was great for me but not for her. I could see that, but I felt she was not aware of how good her own situation really was.

We had a lot of arguments about her going back to school. We talked about it but never calmly. I never said I was threatened by it, but I sure acted threatened.

What about your sexual relationship?

That's hard to remember. Sometimes it was very nice, sometimes not satisfying. After Vita was born it was practically nonexistent. I never thought of having sex with anyone but my wife. I wanted that to be good just like I wanted everything else to be good. When it didn't happen I just learned to accept it, I congratulated myself on being long-suffering. We never fought about it till after Vita was born.

A few months later, Rachel went to the city for a couple of days. I took her to the bus and as I was coming back I started to think how nice it would be if I had someone to sleep with. And then, suddenly, out of the blue, in this tiny town in a strange country an American girl came knocking on the door. I couldn't believe it. I just flipped over it. That was the only time. I never told Rachel. I was not even ashamed, which is strange, because by my own standards I should have been. I felt good just to be able to have sex with someone.

How did you feel about having a child?

We named her Vita because I expected to draw sustenance from family life. The real essence of my life was to be there no matter what I did outside of the family. I did a fair amount of the daily care. I woke up with her at night; every morning I woke up early to work in the garden; then I would dress Vita and diaper her, though I never handled the shit. Rachel fed her mostly, and I played with her. I spent two or three hours with her a day. I felt pretty confident that I was a good father. Rachel and I agreed on child rearing at that time.

Don is more reticent about his early married days, and in fact remembers less. It is an attitude not atypical of the visiting fathers. His was a more conventional marriage to begin with. He was older when he married and expected a traditional family life, with which his wife went along. The dissatisfaction accumulated slowly and had more to do with Don's inability to throw himself wholeheartedly into an intimate relationship and with his need to prove himself outside of the home in work and other activities than with any specifics of his marital relationship. His three children, born at two-year intervals, his success in his profession, a house in the suburbs, all created a veneer of comfort and stability. When his wife became dissatisfied with the quality of their relationship they sought the usual remedies of joint vacations, followed by marriage counseling. When the situation did not improve, Marylou, his wife, suggested that he move out, but he was very resistant to the idea. He gives the impression that he would have continued in the relationship indefinitely if only

Marylou had been willing to overlook their differences. It is not clear that he knew what he wanted from the marriage or that he knows what he wants from relationships now.

At Marylou's insistence, Don finally agreed to sublet an apartment for the summer, just to give himself some "breathing space." There had been a lot of tension in the house and it was beginning to show in the behavior of the children.

I had no idea what I wanted to do. I was very angry at Marylou for separating me from my children. It was very clear to me that I loved the kids more than I was concerned with the relationship with Marylou. I did not realize then that they were the only people in the world I had a close tie to. That summer I came back to the house early every morning to have breakfast with the children. But Marylou put a stop to that. They came to see me on the weekends, and it was really hard to leave them at the end of the weekend.

In the early days of the separation Don tried to find women who would help him with the child care and make the time with the children feel more like time in an intact family, but that did not work out well. Women who did not have children of their own were not sensitive enough, he felt, to his children's needs. When other children were present it meant whole new sets of relationships to deal with. His children had been used to his undivided attention when he was with them, and they resented the inclusion of another adult.

Bill, too, had difficulty deciding what were the exact issues which undermined his marriage. First, Lisa was unhappy with the time it took for him to complete the house and especially to get her studio ready. He sympathized with her impatience but thought he was doing the best he could. At the same time Bill felt that he did not want his life to be centered around success, achievement, and making money; that was one of the reasons he moved to the country. He thought that perhaps Lisa did not find him ambitious enough. They were beginning to be interested in different things. Finally, it seemed to Bill that Lisa did not want to be married any more, at least not in the "where thou goest, I go" way of marriage he had always imagined.

Yet the divorce still was hard to imagine.

I wanted to solve our problems, but that was one solution that had not occurred to me.

Life became more snappy and dissatisfied, but she was also pregnant, and Bill blamed her moods on her condition. After their daughter was born, Bill had to go briefly back to the city to visit his mother, who had been ill. When he returned he realized that some change had taken place with Lisa. Being alone with the child for the month he was away made her not want to live with him any more. The shock of that demand made them talk honestly to each other for the first time.

. . . It was a release. Now we are very close in some ways. It was what we needed to be able to talk to each other and about ourselves.

At that point the baby was less than a year old. They had no place to go so they both stayed in the house. That's when the tension really began to build up. Bill was critical of the way Lisa took care of the baby. Lisa had an affair with another man, and Bill was her confidant. Since both were self-employed, they shared child care. The baby, in fact, kept them with each other beyond the time they might otherwise have stayed together.

The baby was treated very well and taken seriously—but there was something missing. We did not really appreciate her existence—she was considered a burden. Yet it was very easy for me not to express any resentment. I had always been taught to do so. Also both parents were very supportive of me. My parents just said that Lisa had always been very hard to get to know. They thought she was disturbed.

For Larry's marriage, too, it was an accidental separation that made a deliberate separation a real possibility for his wife. It was precipitated by a trip his wife made back home.

What happened then?

Well, I guess when we were married about five years, living in this village, Rachel's aunt died and she went back to the states for six weeks to be with her mother. We were sending each other tapes and I could tell from them that something was wrong. She was not affectionate. I was sending her love letters and I was getting back descriptions of what she was doing.

We talked on the phone and she said she had decided to go back to school and wanted me to come back to help her. I knew something was wrong. Her parents sent me a ticket and when I got off the plane . . . what a shock! She had cut her long hair, she no longer wore a wedding ring and as soon as we got to the house she said she wanted a divorce. She just did not want to be married any more. I had not expected *that!* I was determined not to let it happen. We went to a marriage counselor and decided to try a separation for two weeks. I kept thinking she would come to her senses and everything would be good again.

I took Vita so Rachel could study and went to stay with some friends. I had not planned on staying in the USA at all. But I was not going to go back alone. We went to my folks for a while, then back East so Rachel could continue in school. At first I stayed with a cousin, but then Rachel agreed to try again and we all moved in together. Except that she did not want to have sex with me. She was willing to stay married but would not go back to Mexico. So I cancelled all my commitments there and we were dependent on her relatives until I found another job.

How do you view this in retrospect?

I can see that she was making the best decision for what she wanted to do. We could have gone back and made some modifications, but it would not have been good for her.

When we moved to the city, we found an apartment and I got a job as a youth worker. I was not too good at it at first, but now I'm really good with adolescents.

How was your marriage once you settled here?

We didn't really know how to be nice to each other, how to ask for what we needed. We couldn't share the good stuff. She decided that our spiritual discipline was sexist and wouldn't have anything to do with it. I was, and still am, very much into spirituality. That was one of the major tensions. It did not have to be, I was not so traditional, but it is good to be because it was one of my own main sources of strength and pleasure, and she would not even try to share it. There was a constant threat that she would leave.

We settled down in September and by the end of December she left. We did get along in some ways, had the same sense of humor, liked the same things, but it just was not enough, there was no growth.

Rob sees the birth of their child as a real turning point in the marriage, and seems to blame himself for not being able to come to the aid of his wife. After all, Rob was attracted to Beth because of her energy and vivacity, yet he was not really able to sympathize or help when she felt overburdened and limited by motherhood.

I think we both had trouble dealing with our negative feelings about having a child. It took away our freedom. I think I was overly loving and jolly with the baby to compensate for my anger.

All in all it was a horrible, horrible year. I was under pressure to succeed in my new job. Beth was lonely, overwhelmed by all the responsibility and by living in a strange town. Sometimes I'd come home and find her crying. She tried to talk to me about it but I guess I was not very good at hearing her out. That started Beth working things out on her own because I was not much help to her emotionally.

What happened then?

I think I let Beth down a lot that first year with the baby and she decided she had to do something on her own or she'd go mad. She started a play group among some other young mothers so she could have some time off from child care. Then she found a part-time job and put pressure on me to take more child-care time. Sometime around 1968 the women's movement happened and it had a major impact on our lives. Beth was swept up in it, and almost all the people we knew. The women were putting a lot of pressure on their husbands and I desperately wanted to be accepted as a "good" person with "good" politics. So I did everything I could to be helpful and shoved under the rug conflicts that arose in me. I felt I would have to let go of my professional ambitions and yet could not quite believe that it was happening to me. I did a lot of housework too, but I felt less and less close to Beth.

With the women's movement Beth found an outlet for her energy.

We talked less and less and saw each other less and less. Our sex life really deteriorated. I tried to talk to others about it, but I had always been a loner, so it was hard.

In a move not unusual for couples in trouble, Beth and Rob had a second child when Rob Jr. was four. Their marriage was on the rocks and Rob had a short affair while Beth was pregnant. He told her about it and she was furious. Rob was feeling increasingly trapped and he and Beth withdrew into their separate worlds. Yet their decision was to stay together for the time being and to make some living arrangements which would ease their lifestyle.

What about your sexual relationship?

Beth and I were both eager to experiment sexually. We also both had very limited experience, but we were embarrassed about it and didn't talk about it very much. We wanted to be seen as very worldly. So there was a lot of fumbling; in fact, I think we never got it together sexually. That was one of the weak points in the fabric of our marriage. I was very anxious about sex. I think we both sort of felt that there should be more to it. Well, I do have a memory of an incredibly happy and exciting sexual experience shortly after we were married, and I also remember some horrible times when one person would make a tentative, half-advance, wanting the other person to pick it up and then resented it because you didn't know whether they wanted to or were just trying to be nice and responsive. I remember that happening frequently with Beth and me after we were married.

When did you decide to have children?

Well, like I said before, we had decided not to have children for a while. I had a strong hankering to be an intellectual, a scholar, a writer and to get recognition for that, I knew that would take dedication and discipline. I spent every second I could working when I was in school. I resented Beth's pressure to spend time with her. I gave in a lot, but I really would have preferred to be studying. Rob Jr. was born when we had been married for five years. I guess Beth thought it was time, and I guess I did not have good enough arguments against it. It changed everything. It coincided with my finishing graduate school and moving. We didn't know anybody here and it was a very hard time. I was even more reluctant to take time off from work than I was before. If I helped in the house at all it was because Beth really put the screws on to squeeze it out of me. I didn't really believe that she needed my help. I saw her as a very competent person. She would get up in the morning with fifty things to do and do most of them by the end of the day.

I didn't really know how to act with a baby, I overstimulated Rob Jr., expecting too much of him, and I would not leave him alone. But I was only home evenings and weekends.

Breaking Up

Rob and Beth moved into young faculty housing where they became close with another couple with a child. This living situation suited Rob with his tendency to be accommodating and cooperative better than it suited Beth. She sometimes found herself at odds with the neighbors. Rob, besides participating fully in being a "good husband-provider" made some male friends outside the house. Their married life continued to deteriorate.

I was desperately looking around for a woman at that time. Funny that I did not admit it because it was obvious to anyone. There were two women that I was interested in and I made a pretty obvious play for both of them. Neither was interested in getting embroiled in this thing with me and Beth—they were smarter than that. My feelings about it were very confused and I was desperate. I felt so generally lousy that chasing after women did not make me feel worse. After a while I did become involved with Anna. She had a child about the same age and her marriage, too, was not working out well. So we consoled each other.

After a year in the house, Beth moved out. By that time she and Rob had been married ten years and had two children, aged two and six. They decided on a fifty-fifty arrangement with the kids; Rob still had the assistance of their close neighbors for his child care.

How was it when the children were with you?

I felt very close to the children and would be disoriented when they were not with me. My view of what a good life and a good family meant was very traditional—mom, dad, and the kids at home—my failure to maintain that made me miserable. Beth and I competed a lot for the children's affection at first. If they came back to my house from Beth's in a good mood, I worried that they would not be happy with me. If they were in a bad mood, I'd think that that's because they had to leave her house and come to me. I still do that a little bit. It shows my insecurity at being a good parent, and my assumption that Beth does everything perfectly. That twice-a-week change is still the hardest thing for all of us.

No matter how painful the last months or even years of a marriage have been, the time immediately following separation is almost always remembered as the most difficult time of all. Larry's description best exemplifies the prevalent sense of disorientation and despair. Time spent with the children served to pull some of the fathers out of their depression.

I happened to be off from work for Christmas vacation when she left, so I did nothing. I spent my time laying on the living room couch, drinking, smoking, crying, reading science fiction magazines. It was a great relief to me when I learned a long time later that it's OK to react that way, I didn't know that it was common. I felt very sad and ashamed. It was clear that she left me, and I felt it was my failure to be a good husband and father which was such a large part of who I was.

I was tremendously angry for at least a year, depressed and angry and ashamed. I related to everyone on the basis of the breakup of my marriage. I went to friends and a couple of therapists.

When did you begin to feel like a single person; how did you start to meet other women again?

Well, we both used to like to dance and there was a disco that we used to go to. It was a nice friendly place, it functioned like a singles' bar but you didn't have a feeling of such a heavy scene. I dance well and it was easy to get people to dance with me; sometimes they would even ask me. One time I went and Rachel was there. I couldn't bring myself to approach her. We were both dancing; then I saw her standing in a long embrace with this guy, and she knew that I was there. I just started to cry right in the middle of this bar. She sent one of her women friends to sit with me. Finally I calmed down and left.

That night was a sort of crisis. I wanted to do violence. To murder her. Then I thought, why her? She's happy, alive, it's me. I should kill myself. After about a month I met a woman I liked, but I could not stop thinking about Rachel. I would make love with my friend but be thinking about Rachel.

And then a short time after that I went to a party, and again . . . small world, Rachel was there. She seemed to be having a good time with other people. But I considered myself married; it was just that my wife had left me. That night at the party I thought, if Rachel is making it with other men and I didn't have anybody, then it would spoil our chances of getting back together. So I was dancing with this woman and she seemed nice so I said, "Do you want to come home with me?" And she did. It was really a deliberate decision on my part. It was not based on what I felt like doing but on what I thought was needed to get us back together. I spent a week or two seeing this woman, but I didn't really want to be with her. A month later I met someone I liked, but I could not stop thinking about Rachel. I would make love with my friend, but be thinking about my wife.

How did you feel about yourself?

Well, it was very confusing. Rachel was supposed to be my soulmate, my identity. If she was not happy it meant I wasn't a good husband. If I was not a good husband, then I was just a no-good son-of-a-bitch. All my close friends were very family oriented. Rachel would not do anything to make the marriage work and she would not participate in the things I cared about. We had almost nothing left to share and were always angry at each other. She thought I was a male chauvinist, and I thought I was killing myself staying in the city for her and it meant nothing to her.

Did you think about getting divorced?

Divorce meant failure. It never even came into my mind to divorce her, even after she put me through hell. It would have meant a tremendous loss of face to me, both to myself and to others. I felt we had shared things that I could not share with any other person. I could not imagine what the alternatives to living together might be. When she finally left me I was ashamed to see people. I was even ashamed to walk down the street.

At least I had Vita. She stayed with me, because Rachel wasn't sure she wanted her and I knew I did. But then, when Rachel got a place of her own and she wanted to take Vita with her, I didn't want to give her up. I felt a lot of resentment, even though it was not easy living alone with a child. I had taken care of her before, but it was always when I chose to and not when she needed it.

It was my therapist who finally prevailed upon me to let Rachel have Vita with her. I had her for one and a half days a week. Later we changed to half weeks. We negotiated and cooperated on that, so I am now in a good position with the court. The nagging is over and both of us have now cooperated over child care for two years.

How was it when Vita was with you?

It was hard having her in an everyday sense. It was the responsibility of looking after her when I myself felt like shit. I knew I could take care of her; it was just that I felt lousy. On the other hand it probably saved me to have someone so alive to care for and to love.

What was the most difficult of child care?

The overwhelming sense of responsibility was hard. I gave her a tremendous amount of mothering, partly because Rachel was not into that. She wanted Vita to grow up as fast as possible. I compensated by spending too much time with her, laying too heavy a trip on myself. Rachel always dealt with Vita's clothes—she still does—but I share everything else.

What was the best part?

Vita has pulled out the best in me, the loving parts. Sometimes she just cries with no real reason; she just wants to cry and I let her. I know how to be with her.

Don, too, suffered from displacement and disorientation and looked to his children for some source of support and stability.

They were really there for me. When I would come to the house they would greet me and make me feel really welcome. It was really hard for me; it would bring up feelings of anger at Marylou because it was my house and I couldn't live there anymore. It gave me a mixed feeling of joy and sadness. When it was time to leave, then I would feel just terrible and very alone.

Monday morning was the worst; it was very hard to get up. I'd lay there in bed feeling depressed and immobilized. Sometimes it lasted the whole week. Usually Monday and half of Tuesday, till I got started moving.

What were the hardest things about taking care of the children?

When the kids got sick or something, I felt panicky. If Marylou was around I'd talk to her. Once my son ran a really high fever. I finally called the doctor, but I felt very oppressed by it, that I had to do it all by myself. But luckily there weren't many emergencies.

Sometimes it is also hard to do things with the three of them because of the age differences. Marylou used to complain that the kids were hard to discipline after the weekend. That made me mad because I tried not to be too permissive, I guess they were upset just like I was.

For some years after the separation Don still felt split between his loyalty to the children and his desire to have other relationships, his work, and his friends. He still feels he has not been totally successful in putting it all together.

That feeling of being split in two is still there to some extent. But now I feel less guilty about spending less time with the children. I can also bring them to my house at any time—it does not require any special arrangements.

There were times when I felt guilty about not spending time with the children. That has changed partly because they are growing up. Now, it is the quality of time we spend together that is important. It is not a great tragedy either for them or for me if we don't spend a weekend together. This is less true of the youngest one who still wants to see me a lot and is a drain on me. I try to do things separately with the kids now. It is hard to arrange it that way because Marylou still sees my time with the kids as babysitting for her. She wants to go away for the weekends and then we have a lot of conflict over scheduling. I feel guilty about not staying with them, but I don't want to do it for her. Now I have learned to say to Marylou: this is your problem; it's not between me and the kids.

It is a strain to stay close to the children because I am not there physically. I have either to get it second hand, through Marylou, which may be distorted, or directly from the children, but it's after the fact. I feel that there are times when I don't know what is going on with them, and then I can't be there when they need me. It's a barrier to communications, not living together. But I try to call as frequently as I can and I dig a little into what is happening. I don't feel inadequate or guilty any more.

Rob had the advantage of being the one who stayed put in the house he was living in, while his wife, Beth, moved away. This, together with the support of the friends in his housing development, made the transition of separation much easier for him. Not having to deal with the practicalities of setting up a new household, Rob was better able to concentrate on his feelings and inner states.

After Separation

How did you feel after the separation?

My social life didn't really change because I was already close to Anna. Anna by that time was separated from her husband and living alone also. She wanted to maintain a separate identity. We spent hours and hours talking about what we wanted from each other and what it all meant to us. I also made male friends, but I tended to be reserved with them. My sex life was the main source of reinforcement for me at that time. I felt I had been deprived for so long with Beth, and having a passionate affair with Anna really restored my self-esteem. I felt much freer to be experimenting and adventurous with sex. I didn't worry that Anna would think I was strange. She was interested in fooling around in bed. It was a real boost to my masculinity to feel wanted. The issue that was much harder to change was my conflict between wanting to be free and wanting to accommodate others. It was the same with Anna as it has been with Beth. I always felt that a man should be free to do what he wants, and not to have to consult with a woman. Yet usually I did consult with them and then felt resentful and unmasculine. I'd let the woman have too much power over me and my time. For example, I might feel that I wanted to be alone, but if she wanted to spend time together I just went along. I did not express my resentment over that, but I'd shcw it by forgetting an appointment or some other indirect way. Now I'm working on trying to understand that—being able to express what I want and then working out a compromise. I don't want to lose my sensitivity to others, but I want to be myself at the same time. Just learning to express my feelings was hard.

Each of these men worked out his own way of making arrangements about child care. Larry wanted full custody of his daughter, settled for joint care, but is now facing the possibility of a custody struggle since his wife would like to move out of state and take the child with her. He feels that his history of cooperative child care will help him present his case in court if it comes to that.

Rob has remained in the same house and is now in a stable relationship with the woman he became involved with at the time his marriage was breaking up. He has begun to explore his talent as an artist, something that he previously only used to amuse the children. And he has discovered that by making a modest living as an illustrator, supplemented by a part-time teaching job, he can get the time flexibility he wanted, both to take care of his children and to lead a more family oriented, self-expressive life which he had come to value. His ex-wife has recently remarried, and the pattern of shared child care seems to continue amicably.

Don has gone through a succession of relationships with other women. He no longer tries to integrate his life as a father with these relationships. With time he has become more self-sufficient emotionally, but still retains a strong connection with his children. He sees them on the average of once every week, and would still like to remarry if the "right" person came along.

Bill is one of the joint-care fathers. Since his wife has remained in the country and he has moved to the city, the time periods during which he has his daughter vary. They have experimented with a month at a time and six months, and plan to try alternating years. The arrangement depends on their work and on their daughter's school situation. Both feel that their child is now an integral part of their lives and can be easily fitted into it. Bill and his ex-wife still have a very "civilized" relationship and feel confident that they can resolve any practical child-care problems as they arise.

CHAPTER 3

Fathers Who Take Care of Children

The present study examines the lifestyles of separated fathers who maintain regular contact with their young children after marital separation. Our criteria for accepting men into the study were that each father should spend at least two days a month with his child, that at least one of the children be no older than seven, and that the separation occurred at least one year prior to the interview. The criterion of at least a year of separation was important since we were interested in researching child-care schedules which had been arrived at after some consideration and had the possibility of stability; we had discovered from previous studies that the first year of separation is an unstable time when men experiment with new lifestyles and experiences. The presence of young children in the family was also an important criterion, since they always require a good deal of parental attention while older children vary greatly in the amount of time and energy they require from their parents.

Interviewing Procedures

Once our sample had been selected, each man was interviewed with the aid of a structured interview form. The interviews took two to two and a half hours. Each respondent was also asked to complete a form which examined sex-role attitudes and gender-related self-concept (see Appendix A). Ten of the fathers were selected for a more detailed case study, and each of these was interviewed in open-ended sessions for a total of eight to ten hours per subject. These long interviews served as a guide for the researchers to develop techniques for structured interview as well as to the deeper feelings and background experiences behind many of the short responses. All case-study material was taped and subsequently coded.

The ten case studies were conducted by Dr. Keshet; the remainder of the subjects were interviewed by trained male interviewers (twelve in all), who were graduate students or graduates of social science, social work, or education programs. All interviewers were men between the ages of twenty-five and thirty-four. In an attempt to establish maximum conditions for rapport, we were concerned that the interviewers have the maturity and sensitivity to be able to probe in an emotional area of investigation. Six of the interviewers were themselves fathers of young children. The interviewers arranged meeting times, and the interviews generally took place at the father's house on weekends or in the evenings.

The interviewers participated in two training sessions. Each had an opportunity to conduct three training interviews, and a meeting was held three weeks after the initial training to discuss their subsequent experiences. The interviewers were in close contact with the project directors throughout the study. Their major problem was scheduling interview time, as many of the men had heavy time commitments. The interview itself was often quite emotional, many of the fathers wanted to talk more than the allotted time; some men talked for three or four hours. Many said that the interview helped them to focus on issues of parenting which they had not considered before and that they learned new things about themselves and their children.

After the data was collected a code was developed for the open-ended questions, and all the coding was done by the project codirectors.

Our study was exploratory and guided both by our previous research on part-time fathers and by insights from other studies on separated and divorced fathers. Keeping the father role as our central focus, we divided the questionnaire into the following areas: the father-child relationship and parenting activities; the relationship between fathers and ex-spouse; and parenting in relation to self-identity, work, social life, future marriage and future paternity. We also gathered information concerning marital history, family parenting experiences, residency and dwelling composition, SES, custody and alimony payments and social and emotional support systems for parenting. A set of open-ended questions allowed the respondents to define categories of responses.

Sample Selection

Identifying a sample of men with a child no older than seven and with half- or full-time child-care obligations presented a difficult problem. The details of our sample selection procedure presented below might serve to provide some measure of insight into that rather unusual population, and might be of use to future researchers.

COURT RECORDS

We had originally assumed that court records would provide us with the best source for finding divorced fathers, and that by sampling several court districts we would maximize the randomness and heterogeneity of our respondents. We began by reviewing all court summaries of divorce cases for the three years preceding the study. Although such summaries are supposed to include the father's address, the number and age of the children and custody disposition, we found that the summaries were often incomplete and that changes in the custody arrangements subsequent to the original hearings were often not recorded; in many of the cases the custody decisions were recorded as pending. We were able to identify only seventy-five cases where the divorcing father met our criteria in terms of age of child and custody arrangements. A letter explaining the study and containing a form to be completed and a stamped return envelope was mailed to each of these seventy-five names.

Forty-three of the seventy-five letters mailed were returned unopened marked "addressee unknown" or "moved, left no forwarding address." Even though we were aware from our previous research of the general instability of the first post-divorce year, we had assumed that these men, particularly if they had custody of small children, would have more continuity in their lives in terms of living arrangements. We had no way of checking whether the letters not returned to us ever reached their destination. Only three of the letters yielded a return, and these men were included in the sample.

Next, we attempted to locate the men whose letters were returned undelivered by looking up their names in the phonebooks of their own and surrounding communities. We located twelve names. All were contacted by phone, and five turned out to be the men we were seeking. Of those five only one met the study criteria. (Three others had remarried, and one had given up the custody of the children.) This experience would make us wary of any claims by other researchers of obtaining a random or representative sample of this population. The very ability to locate the divorced fathers implies a degree of stability which is more likely to be found among the economically comfortable middle-class men grounded in their careers or communities than a random population.

DAY-CARE CENTERS

Given the small returns from our court record search and the high cost of pursuing this avenue of sample identification, we next turned to day-care centers, since most fathers with responsibility for small children rely heavily on such services. We discussed our project with the staff of Child Care Resource

Center in Cambridge and gained their cooperation and entrance into day-care centers affiliated with them. In all, we visited forty-five day-care centers in the Greater Boston area and thirty-nine of them agreed to distribute our forms to the single fathers of their client children. The Centers mailed the forms for us to all fathers who had a separate residence. This included, therefore, informally separated as well as divorced fathers. Even then, out of a mailing of 276 letters, twenty were returned marked "addressee unknown." We received forty-two responses from men willing to participate in the study, of which twenty-seven met the criteria of the study.

LAWYERS

In the course of our involvement with the project we had been in touch with several lawyers who specialized in handling custody cases for fathers. These lawyers offered to refer to us fathers who met the criteria of the study. We followed the same procedures as with the day-care centers. Seven lawyers handed our forty-six letters to their clients, describing the study. Of those, eleven were returned by men who became a part of the sample.

OTHER ATTEMPTS

As locating young fathers became increasingly difficult, we decided to change our strategy by appealing to the men directly. We began to advertise for full-time, half-time and biweekly visiting fathers. We hoped to get a better return rate by providing phone contact rather than a form that had to be completed and mailed.

A tape discussing the study was played at intervals by a local radio station, and those interested were given an answering service number to call. All calls were then returned, and the callers were checked for eligibility and willingness to cooperate. Additionally, announcements in various organizational news-letters and a leaflet describing the project and asking for volunteers to call were widely distributed and posted in day-care centers, supermarkets, laundries and churches throughout the Boston metropolitan area. In all, one hundred and twenty men called about the study, and of those, fifty-three became respondents.

And finally, we asked each man interviewed if he knew of any other fathers in the same situation. This question served a twofold purpose. It gave us potential additional respondents, and it helped us to gauge a measure of support and self-help network that might be available to the men from others in the same situation. Thirty-three names were obtained in this manner, of which seventeen became our respondents. In all, sixty-seven of the respondents were self-referred (53 percent) and sixty (47 percent) were identified by another individual or organization. Of all the men who were contacted and who fitted the study criteria, only two refused to be interviewed.

A major characteristic of the men in our sample was their willingness and voluntary cooperation. Since respondents were paid only a small amount for their participation, monetary gain could not have been a major motivating force for participation. Fathers seemed to be giving their evening or weekend time as a means of expressing personal concern and interest in their parenting activities.

Men with differing child-care schedules came to the study through different avenues. For example, full-time fathers were most likely to be referred by courts or agencies, or even by extended family members (a sister of one of our respondents phoned to say what a "heroic job" her brother was doing in being a full-time parent); half-time fathers, being less visible to courts and social service agencies, were most likely to be referred by other fathers (or call in themselves). Those fathers whose parenting contact was limited to biweekly visits were a more easily identified and more numerous group, and we had no trouble finding them in any divorced population. Few of these men, however, could be found through day-care centers or other agencies, indicating that their involvement with their children did not generally extend to those networks.

Group Profiles

As noted previously the interviews were designed to explore several different areas of the fathers' lives: the relationship with the children and parenting activities; relationship with ex-spouse, the attitudes towards parenting as they related to the father's self-identity, his work, social life and future life plans.

Taking as our main variable the amount of time that the men in our sample spent with their children, we divided the fathers into four groups: full-time fathers (49); joint-custody or half-time fathers, whose child-care time was divided equally with their ex-spouses (29); men who took care of their children no less than seven days each month, but not quite half-time (21); and finally fathers who generally spent every other weekend with their children for a total of no more than six days a month (28). Although as we will see there were some significant differences among these groups, it must be remembered that all these men are *distinctive* in that they are a *frequent presence* in the lives of their children. We can assume however, that all the men in our sample have made deliberate decisions about their parental ties and that the details of their arrangements are an expression of their particular circumstances and attitudes. We don't know how many divorced men in the general population who see their children only rarely would prefer more frequent contact if the psychological or practical circumstances of their lives made such arrangements feasible. Men in our sample were both able and willing to make child rearing a significant part of their lives after marital separation. We realize that they are unusual.

Although national statistics indicate that only approximately 17 percent of all divorcing men ask for custody of their children, and that of these only 65 percent are awarded custody by the courts, most divorced men who desire to maintain parental ties with their children make some formal or informal arrangements for part-time parenting. Aware of the legal system's bias against paternal custody, they are unlikely to bring their case to court unless they can present a very convincing argument on their own behalf. Thus the frequency of the legal custody requests by fathers does not represent the true picture of the desire or willingness on the part of the fathers to take over the care of their children.

In addition, the available social roles, norms and expectations made explicit by the legal proceedings, and the assumed obligations of fatherhood, provide little support for daily parenting roles for men. The courts are more approving of the father who works long hours away from home to support his estranged wife and children than of the one who asks for more time with the children at the risk of lessening his income. Despite the previously outlined arguments about the importance of the father's involvement in the development of children, the divorce system is geared primarily to protecting the society from the economic burden of a dependent mother and the couple's children.

The following descriptions highlight some of the differences we found among the four groups of fathers. The descriptions are based on the group averages and it must be remembered that not every man in each group conforms to these norms.

I—THE OCCASIONAL FATHER

Although on the whole the men we interviewed were young men with young children, the occasional father tends to be older than the rest of our sample and is also likely to come from a more conservative background. This father is a regular and helpful visitor, but views his role mainly as that of a provider and an authority. In this he feels he is similar to his concept of what is typical for men in general.

His visiting schedule is more likely to be biweekly, for one day or a weekend. He says that he was close to his children before the separation but that his main difficulty as a parent is lack of patience, particularly in handling the emotional aspects of child care. "It's when I don't know why she's crying," said one father, "that I get to feel helpless and inadequate."

When the visiting father spends time with his children, he is most likely to look for ways to entertain them. He is concerned that it is hard for him to find time for his children and feels that he is not emotionally suited for the kind of activities that small children enjoy. Many of the visiting fathers anticipated that the relationship with their children would improve as the child got older.

The visiting fathers were most likely to have two children, a boy and a girl, with the girl being the older. It is difficult to say in a sample of this size whether the particular sibling order we have found to prevail in each group is simply an accident of sampling. We might speculate, however, that the sex of the oldest child sets a certain model for the parenting relationship and that men whose first child is male might become more involved in the parenting process from infancy, while fathers of daughters may feel less able to make a contribution to early child care.

Although the ex-wives are good at keeping them informed about their children, these fathers report that mothers often interfere with their relationships with the children. It is not that the mother keeps them from the children, but that she is apt to try to mediate their relationships. There is also often a high degree of conflict between the ex-spouses, usually focused on the issue of money. These men tend to be more deprecating than the others in our sample in describing their ex-wives' character. They disagree particularly about child-rearing techniques, especially discipline, but they appear wary about open conflict since they depend on the their ex-wives to facilitate their contact with the children.

These men are most likely of all the men in the sample to be living alone, although many of them have close female friends with whom they spend a great deal of time. When the children are with him, the visiting father is likely to spend most of the time away from his residence, since it is not really set up for children except for a few toys or books. His woman friend may accompany him on these excursions. She is likely to be single with no children of her own and is often very helpful to him with his child care. She is less likely, however, to share child care with the father at his own house. This area of parenting is jealously guarded for him alone.

Men in this group as well as the full-time fathers, most desire remarriage. Many wish to have full custody of the children, but only under conditions of remarriage. They are moderately satisfied with their lifestyle, and cite child-care arrangements and personal relationships as major sources of concern. Some of the fathers are quick to express resentment at their ex-wives and wish that the situation could be reversed and they could be the custodial parent while the mother provided financial support. They see the two functions as incompatible.

In the area of work, these men tend to excell. They work full-time or more, and their income is substantially higher than the incomes of the younger men who spend more child-care time.

It is our conclusion from careful reading of the interview material that these men have strong images of family life and wish to maintain close ties to their children. But they are unwilling to make major changes in their lifestyles to accomplish this end. Their activities with their children are the same as before separation: taking them to restaurants, playgrounds and entertainment. The time they spent with their children is the traditional father's "free" time, weekends and holidays. They feel comfortable with their fathering inasmuch as it continues the predivorce situation. Although many of these men have told us that the experience of single fathering has made them more responsible and self-aware, they cannot easily imagine an increased involvement in their children's lives without the setting of a conventional two-parent family. Therefore, they tend to mourn their broken marriage and express more resentment towards their ex-spouses.

2—THE QUARTER-TIME FATHER

This second group of fathers ranges over a variety of visiting schedules. Most of the men see their children more than once a week but do not have the strict half-time schedule which characterizes the joint-custody father. These men tended to have two children, the older one being a boy. As mentioned before, the fact of the first child's gender may have influenced the father's feeling of closeness to the children and hence his desire for increased time with his children. Many of the fathers have said that the postdivorce time spent with the children has forged a special bond between them. There is a paradox there that underlines the complexity of the child-father bond. For example, although men in this group tend to be least at ease with the emotional issues of child rearing and frequently report responding with anger and annoyance to their children's temper tantrums or other "irrational" behaviors, yet they are less likely to be authoritarian in their dealing with the children. When faced with discipline problems they often react with guilt and fear and find it difficult to enforce rules of behavior for their children. Frequently, they are likely to have their children all or part of every weekend and for some period in between weekends. The father's residence has whatever is necessary to make the children comfortable and a part of his household. Although some of these men maintain a residence of their own, most are likely to share their dwelling with male roommates. The quarter-time father is more likely than the rest of the men to date women who are divorced and have children of their own. He is likely to spend the time he is not with his children in the company of his friend and her family. Since these men date mothers, the women are less likely to be present when the children are visiting. Most often the father will avail himself of the help of paid sitters or friends and see his woman friend when they are both child-free. The high level of contact with others, including his children, friends, lovers and the children of others, gives the quarter-time father a characteristic of sociability.

Many of the quarter-time fathers feel that their wives withhold information from them about the children, and are likely to be ones who initiate contact with the ex-wife in order to keep themselves involved with the children. Although their wives are flexible about child-care arrangements, and many men have availed themselves of that flexibility in making changes in the child-care schedules, it appears that what they gain in flexibility they lose in a sense of control of their lives with the children. This is in contrast to the half-time fathers who, by their strict adherence to the schedule, even at some inconvenience to themselves, are able to make demands for participation and sharing of information, and get more willing cooperation from their ex-spouses. It may be, as we discuss later, that the quarter–time fathers are still in a transitional stage of establishing their parenting role. The high degree of conflict and ambivalence about the ex-wives may be a sign of an unresolved relationship which underlies their group's lack of desire to remarry.

It may also be that these men, like the occasional fathers of the previous group, are fixated on the conventional images of their male role. For them any behavior that requires "mothering" the children, while necessary to maintain the contact, emphasizes the role conflicts and painfully recalls the marital disruption. During marriage, these men did a great deal with their children, and so they wish to continue that role, but feel very deprived of the supports which a married lifestyle provided. It may well be that they seek women who have had the experience of being wives and mothers. Yet their continued involvement in their present family configuration and the energy it absorbs makes the thought of remarriage difficult.

3—THE HALF-TIME FATHER

The half-time father is striking for the low reported level of conflict with his ex-wife. He does not rely on her much for child-care assistance, and gets a great deal of help from friends, roommates and others. He also tends to have less personal contact with his ex-wife. The schedule with the children tends to be rigidly divided into some half-time arrangement, either by weeks or half-weeks. Thus he often takes the children to school and picks them up from school, rather than from the mother's house, eliminating what all men describe as an uncomfortable encounter.

This father is significantly different from men in the other group by having only one child of school or day-care age, and that child is likely to be male. Although he is probably separated rather than divorced, his child-custody arrangements are often legal rather than informal and thus he feels more secure in his rights as a father. Since he usually pays little or no child support money to the mother, (providing direct support instead) a whole other potential area of conflict between him and his ex-spouse is eliminated. His house is definitely set up to include living with children. Space, supplies and work schedules are all oriented around the child's life. He is very aware of the limitation that child care places on his work time and energy, and feels very committed to having increased services such as day care or flexible work hours.

This father is more likely than the others to live with unrelated adults and perhaps own his own home. He is a social person and dates a great deal. The women he dates, or is likely to associate with, are single and do not have children of their own, yet many of his activities are home-oriented whether with or without the children. And he and his date are just as likely to stay at home whether the children are with them or not. The time that the children are with him is more distributed over a series of activities; the children may play by themselves or with playmates, or watch TV, as well as spend time with the father alone.

The regular schedule allows for the cultivating neighborhood friends, and since school, or day care, is the focal pick-up point, many half-time fathers make it a point to live within a convenient distance from the day care, and the child is able to be in contact with the network of friends from either parent's house. Although his own contact with his ex-wife is not defined by the child transfer, he does keep in close touch with her about the matters of the child's daily routine, participates more in all child-related chores and tasks, and thinks well of his ex-wife both as a mother and as a person.

When alone with the child, this father does low-key activities, such as talking, or walking together, and relies less on structured entertainments. This is partly because his home and lifestyle are set up for such activities with children, and partly, perhaps, because this is not a high-income group and outside entertainment constitutes an added expense.

Perhaps because the father himself is more home oriented, perhaps because his dates are likely to be single and not experienced with children, and finally, perhaps because there is often just one child to take care of, this father is not likely to rely on his lover to take his place. Her contact with the child is limited, and there is not the sense that he relies on her, or other women, to help him in the child care. Although these fathers come from a highly educated group, their work lives are somewhat limited by the child-care obligations, with the atten-dant limits on income, job mobility and promotions. Yet this group of fathers has the highest reported satisfaction with their lifestyle. They also appear to have made a choice to limit their economic and work mobility rather than their social life as the major cost of child-care responsibilities. These men hold a less rigid male stereotype and express more flexibility in their attitudes towards sex roles and task equality in the home.

It is interesting to note here that there are some striking differences in the quality of the life of the quarter-time and half-time fathers, and yet when we look strictly at the amounts of time spent with the child, the differences are often blurred. The quarter–time father and the half–time father are both often with their children *every weekend*. Both do large amounts of household chores and other child-care tasks for close to half of the time, yet their expressed sense of satisfaction and the general sense of coping is quite different. It seems as if it is not the specifics of the time schedule with the children that accounts for the differences, but rather the way this fathering participation is *defined*. By referring to themselves as "half-time parents" these men are declaring their rights as well as obligations. The picture of equity they present allows them to be freed from child support obligations, which in turn frees them from some of the anxiety about work. By having a clear understanding of their half-time obligations, they structure the child care into their daily lives in such a way that it becomes a part of their life routine and is not a continual disruption. These fathers talk about living half-time with their children, rather than "being stuck with them on the weekend." The child care does not become an extra burden to be fitted in with all their other activities. Their total lives become reoriented, often more home oriented as a result. Living with other adults provides a semblance of family life. The relationship with the ex-wife becomes more mutual. Each has a stake in viewing the other as a "good parent," as long as the other fulfills their time schedule assignment.

The half-time father is comfortable enough with his life that he is not anxious to remarry. (It is interesting to note that he is more likely to be separated for a longer period of time than other types of fathers, and yet less likely to have been legally divorced. If we view divorce as a way for men to regain control in the disrupted marital relationship, it would support the assumption that the issue of control vis-à-vis the ex-wife is less at stake here.)

We might also note again that this father is more likely to have a male child. In fact the proportion of male children increases with the increase in the assumption of care. We do not know whether the fact that their child is male becomes a motivating factor for the fathers to assume parental responsibility, or whether it is a factor in the mother's having social approval, or even pressure, to relinquish some control of the child.

4—THE FULL-TIME FATHER

The full-time father differs from the other group in that his arrangement is much less likely to be voluntary. Given the present attitudes and rules concerning custody, it is unlikely that a father can have full custody of his children unless the mother has willingly, or out of necessity, given up her rights to the children. Thus many a father with custody may never have had the opportunity of deciding whether or not he wanted to be the only caretaker of his children. Many of the wives have been unable or unwilling to share the child care. Some of the men had wives who were sick, mentally unstable or alcoholic, and there is a degree of resentment that creeps in when they discuss their former wives.

The full-time father is not likely to live near his wife or rely on her much for child-care assistance. He has arranged his life to take care of the children either by hiring help or by having a helpful lover or friends. Thus his work hours and daily routine are not viewed as limited by child care, but his adult entertainment and social life are. He is just as likely to complain of not enough time with his children as fathers in conventional marriages, and does in fact spend less time with them than the part-time father. He feels the difference between himself and his coworkers and is likely to complain about a lack of understanding from others at work, particularly other men, about his special situation. He, of all other fathers, is most anxious to remarry and tends to date women who are single and childless. His future mate's compatibility with his children matters more to him than to other men. He would consider having more children on remarriage, for reasons that have to do with his own preference rather than the preference of the future mate.

The full-time father's life has stability. He is likely to own his own house and to have lived there for a considerable length of time, since he, having kept the children, may have been the one to stay in the marital residence. Not having the ready assistance of the ex-wife, he tends to rely on social services, individual professionals, and agencies, more than other men do. Perhaps he is also more reliant on his community because of residential stability. Since time spent with his children is after work hours, when he is with them they are all more likely to stay at home.

In spite of the possible unwilling takeover of child care that fathers in this category represent, these men would opt for the same arrangements if they had the choice. More frequently than other groups they report full custody or joint custody as their preferred child-care arrangements.

The full-custody father wishes only that he had been better prepared. And a higher proportion of full-time fathers suggest educational programs which would teach men about child care.

The Process of Becoming a Father Without a Partner

Although the specifics of child-care arrangements differ for these groups, their major themes remain the same. The divorced men are concerned with maintaining a viable part of their parenting role. This means that they must be able to have some power in the parent-child relationship, some control over the major decisions affecting the life of their children, and some possibility of negotiating those issues with their ex-spouses. This process of postdivorce parenting is neither easy nor simple.

The process of becoming a father without a partner begins with accepting the irreversibility of the marital breakup. As long as a man clings to his broken marriage, he will attempt to continue his dependence on his estranged wife in regard to child-care activities, and preseparation family roles will be maintained. However, once he accepts the new situation, he will gradually grow more independent of his former spouse. At the beginning of a couple's separation, it is not uncommon to find the woman continuing to plan the man's time with the children and to monitor their activities. Even when a former spouse does not do this directly, many men continue to act as fathers out of a concern for their ex-wife's approval or disapproval of what the children tell her about their activities with him.

With the loss of the marital setting and the gradual lessening of his attachment to his former wife, the separated or divorced father is able to integrate new points of reference for his parenting activities—namely, other adults, his own growing competence, and the reactions of his children. As he learns to rely on these new resources, he becomes less and less dependent on the internalized voice and actual reactions of his ex-wife. Seeking out and finding new resources to support him in his child-care activities is the beginning of self-reliance for the father. As the recipients of his care and the individuals with whom he is frequently and intimately connected, his children become the major point of reference for his behavior. Gradually, then, the father transfers his need for the validation of his competence as a parent from his former wife to his children. This transfer represents the core of the change from fathering within the marital context to single parenthood, and it is central to new parenting behaviors. The single father begins to adjust his behavior to his perceptions of his children's needs. The skills involved in this process are rarely learned by men as part of their socialization as males in this society.

At the beginning of the transition from married parent to single father, the individual is likely to become dependent to an exaggerated extent on his children's reactions to his behavior. He imbues the children with the power of an authority. He constantly reevaluates his performances on the basis of their responses. Any sign of dissatisfaction on their part is taken by him as a personal rejection and as proof of his parental inadequacy. In other words, since he lacks internal standards for his success as a father, he depends on his children's reactions to enable him to define his role. In the traditional parent-child relationship, children learn from their parents; at this time, fathers learn their new role from their children.

By identifying with the children, he comes to share the emotional authority with which he has imbued them. At first he projects his own fears and insecurities onto them, but as his acute anxiety over the separation diminishes and he begins to feel more competent as a parent, he is able to differentiate between his feelings and fears and the realities of his children's experience. The fact that he has responsibility for his children's care provides physical and emotional structure for both himself and the children. Child-care tasks become more predictable and routine. Moreover, cooking meals, cleaning house, bathing the children, and responding to their requests serve as proof to him of his parental adequacy and, by extension, of his personal adequacy. At the same time, he learns that to do these tasks well, he must take care of himself. Creating a comfortable and secure environment for his children means creating one for himself. Respecting his children's emotional and physical needs means respecting his own needs too. This new priority of taking care of themselves is the beginning of maturity for many men for whom responsibility had meant self-denial. As Parsons has commented, "Dependency and maturity is guided by the nature of that which must be cared for." (Parsons, 1964).

The man who is able to recognize his dependence on his children's love, as well as their dependence on his care and attention, and who can rally his emotional energy to respond to his children despite his own sense of crisis and deprivation, will find that the parental relationship is the definitive reference point for restructuring his lifestyle, his behavior, and his self-concept. In learning to take care of his children's needs, he learns to take care of his own. Erikson has indicated that the parenting relationship is an important stage in the identity formation of adults. Yet many fathers who are parents by biological definition but whose development is determined predominantly by the values and demands of the working world never truly achieve that stage. (Erikson, 1968).

As a father gains a sense of himself, his children emerge for him as individuals in their own right. They are no longer viewed by him as simply being children in the family, nor as the sole source of his self-esteem. Instead of seeing them as part and parcel of the marriage and their needs as being subsumed under the global need to maintain the family, he is now able to act toward them in a flexible and responsive way. When this differentiation is complete, he will have developed some standards for parenting and should be able to make decisions on how he will care for the children and how they must, in turn, contend with his individuality. In other words, *their relationship becomes mutual.*

This progression can be viewed as mirroring the development of ego boundaries. That is, the individual moves from a sense of failure and despondency and from demands that are defined for him by the perimeters of the husbanding role to a situation in which individually determined expectations and routines and a sense of mutual dependence prevail.

To maintain the emotional attachment between himself and his children, a father must develop a sensitivity to them. In doing so, he is again faced with their dependency needs, their feelings of powerlessness and impotence, their emotionality, and their irrationality. He must face these factors not only as they are expressed by his children but also as elements that he himself had to suppress during his own childhood as he acquired the veneer of masculinity. By identifying with his children he reexperiences these emotions; by realizing his power as an adult he has an opportunity to resolve them for himself in new and better ways.

Many fathers in the subsample reported that they became angry when their children cried for no immediately discernible reason. At such times they may be seeing their children as irrational and unmanageable, for the children may be expressing emotions that the fathers never learned to manage or control:

I did not listen to my child; I used to get mad when he cried just because he was sad. Then I realized that my father never let me do that, so I was not allowing my child to experience it either.

Understanding his own responses has helped this father become aware of the prescription controlling his own behavior, and of its source. But more important, he realizes he is free to allow his child to behave differently. He therefore can free himself as well. By attending to his children, the separated or divorced father can become his own child and his own parent. By identifying with and being responsible for his children, he can get in touch with the internalized standards dictating his own behavior and, at the same time, see himself as an effective agent for changing them. Thus, men who have separated from or divorced their wives, and have taken on some major responsibility for their children's care, find that the demands of that responsibility can become an important focus for their own growth.

CHAPTER 4

The Case for Co-Parenting

In the following pages we have outlined some of the stages, problems and solutions that characterize the evolving experience of divorced men. The case of John, Abby, and Cynthia represents a composite of the lives of many of the men we interviewed. It is a vivid way of illustrating the many dimensions of the life of a separated father, which we have learned from our subjects.

John, Abby, and Cynthia

It is Wednesday afternoon, three o'clock. John nervously glances at the clock. He is an attorney in private practice and is in the middle of reviewing an important contract for his client, a large liquor store chain. He has a sense of panic. His secretary is waiting for his final correction of the draft, and he must pick up his child at four from the day-care center. He has been late once before, and the day-care director made it clear that she would not stay beyond 4:00 p.m.

What we are describing is transition on many levels. It is a transition from being a husband-father to being a single parent; a transition from work to child care; and a transition from the childless half-week, Sunday to Wednesday, to his parenting time, Wednesday to Sunday afternoon. For half a week John is single, with all the freedom and prerogatives of single men. From Wednesday to Sunday he is a parent with the burdens and loneliness of a single parent. He does not forget about Cynthia entirely during his childless time and usually talks with her on the phone at least once during the time she is with her mother.

It is on Wednesdays, when he first sees five-year-old Cynthia after absence, that John is most likely to feel that he has acutely missed her. He wants to hug her and reestablish the intensity of his feelings, but he has learned that he must move more slowly. After not seeing him for a few days Cynthia is likely to be a little shy and stand-offish, she has her own ways of handling the transition which he must learn and respect. So he keeps his distance, asks her about her day, and then suggests that they go to the playground for a half-hour before going home. Cynthia loves the swings there, and as John pushes her, they can talk a little about what she has been doing. Three days can be a long time for a small child, and he needs to be brought up to date on her moods and feelings. Now that the transition has been made he can catch her as she slips off the swing and hug her hello and take her home. He knows he is lucky to have the time and the means to respond to Cynthia's needs.

There are time when John cannot go through this process as easily—times when he is too preoccupied with job worries or with other personal concerns. Then there is no time for the playground, no energy for careful attention. Sometimes John barely glances at the drawing she proudly displays, or forgets to pick up the knapsack of clothes which she brings to school with her. At those times it may be Cynthia who has to be the sensitive one. She is likely to ask him: "What's wrong Dad, are you mad?" And then he melts. He knows that there is a bond between them, that somewhere the connection has been made, and that his decision not to lose his child to an overload of other obligations has paid off.

COMING HOME

Home is a medium-sized apartment located on a side street in a residential neighborhood. It's a two-family building with a little backyard. There is a family with two children in the other half, and, although the children are somewhat older than Cynthia, they provide her with some company during the summer. Occasionally John can ask the couple next door to listen in for Cynthia after she has gone to sleep, if he goes out in the evening. He does not do that often, or stay out for a long time when he does. He is too worried that something might happen to frighten her during his absence. At other times, he gets a local teenager to babysit. But generally on the days he has Cynthia he stays home. It is easier and less expensive, and besides, he still feels a little uncomfortable calling for a babysitter—something his wife always did when they were married. When he has to call a sitter he has not met before he is particularly worried, perhaps unjustifiably, that he will be treated with suspicion because he is a man.

There is a separate bedroom for Cynthia where she keeps toys, books, and some clothes that she leaves at his house all the time. Her favorite doll and her little baby blanket (which she still uses) come and go with her. All the necessities are provided so that she can stay with John, if need be, on a moment's notice. Her toothbrush stays in the bathroom. John was almost talked into getting her a kitten when the cat next door had a litter, but he decided that that would be a more constant responsibility than he wanted.

John is proud of this apartment and the way he has arranged it. It is a recently acquired competence. In the beginning it was hard for him to feel that he could make a place feel like home. In fact, when he and his wife first broke up, he got a room for himself, which was all he had energy for. But after a while of feeling sorry for himself and feeling totally displaced, he moved in with a group of people he met through a young lawyer friend who was also divorced. It was a large, cheerful house with four room-mates, a dog, and lots of plants. It did feel like home, but not *his* home. He liked it for a while; there was always someone to talk to, people were sympathetic to his troubles, the rent was low, and, when Cynthia was with him and he wanted to go out, there was usually someone in the house to mind her.

But as time went by and he got into his child-care routine, it worked less and less well. Although other adults in the house said they would help him with child care, in fact he did not feel free to ask them, and they were often not sensitive to what needed to be done. Besides, he was concerned about Cynthia's reaction to a lot of strangers, so he tried to take care of her himself. At the same time, the free coming and going of the other adults, their late mornings when he had to get up early to get his daughter off, or late evenings when he wanted her to get to sleep early, began to make him feel even more lonely. Finally, there was the problem of space. First Cynthia shared a room with him, then with the child of his friend who visited his father on weekends. But after a while none of this seemed satisfactory.

John wanted privacy to be with his daughter when he had her, and a different kind of privacy when he was alone. A year after separation he decided that he was strong and secure enough to search for the new home he wanted, and to fix it up the way he wanted to live. He found an apartment that was close enough both to Cynthia's day care and to his ex-wife's house. (It was still hard not to say *his house*—his name was still on the mortgage—though he had not lived there for over a year.) It was clean and light, and had two bedrooms and a study. There would be a room for Cynthia and even extra work space for himself.

I liked getting set up. I spent the weekends painting, doing floors, building cabinets; I built a loft bed for Cynthia so she could store her toys underneath and have more room to play. But the hardest thing was choosing a rug and picking out curtains. That's so lonely to do by yourself. You want another opinion, or someone else who cares. It took a long time before I got it all done. I finally had to ask my secretary. She is an older woman and there is nothing romantic between us, but I had to have someone's help. I guess, really, I had to have a woman's help.

Now, six months later, it does feel like home to John, and he even likes to entertain in his new apartment.

There was another kind of settling in that had to go on as well. John and Cynthia had to find their own space in the apartment: psychological space and private space. It had to be home for both of them, but especially a home for John, because Cynthia had another home as well. That was not how John saw it in the beginning. It was all for Cynthia. He would not need an apartment of his own if it was not for his child; he would not need all that space; even the color of the rug was chosen with her activities in mind.

So in the beginning it was very much a home for Cynthia. When she was not there, neither was John. He ate out or visited friends. When she was there, she used all of it. Her stuff was all over the place, and John never seemed able to keep it in any particular order. When he did things around the house she followed him around, and so did her mess. He wanted to be with her but was beginning to feel like there was no line between him and her. He wanted to be available, but surely this was a bit too much. At that point, John as a father was totally dependent on what his daughter thought of him. If she cried or was unhappy he was a bad father; if she was all smiles he was good. Nothing could be denied her because it reflected badly on him.

John did not know how common that situation was to newly separated fathers, who begin to rely on their children for feedback about their fathering just as they once had depended on their wives. Sometimes John had to remind himself that *he* was the father and *she* was just a little girl who did not know better than he what was good for her. It took a while, but eventually, almost out of a sense of self-preservation, John began to make rules: toys had to stay in her room, except for games they both played; an appropriate children's program could be found that Cynthia could watch while he made dinner, or she could help him and follow his directions. Sometimes, he would have extra work in the evenings and he should not be interrupted. He would then tell her ahead of time that he would have to work for an hour or so and make sure she had everything that she wanted. Perhaps that was somewhat demanding of a five-year-old, but it worked. Cynthia knew that John could be depended on, but would not be available at her beck and call. It made her feel more secure to know that there was an adult in charge. She became less demanding as a result. John was beginning to make boundaries between himself and his daughter which would give them both the space they needed to grow and be alone, while still allowing them to be available to each other.

Living together in small quarters poses problems of intimacy. The underlying issue here for John, as for all separated men, is the issue of competence in the area of parenting alone. Most men view their wives as *the* competent parent, almost by definition, unless she explicitly fails as a parent. Many men identify themselves as "mother's helpers." To be the central parent is both unfamiliar and frightening. The more child care a divorced father undertakes—as the joint-care or full-custody fathers do—the more aspects of child care fall under his supervision. While the weekend father is not likely to be called upon to take his child to the doctor or dentist, or even to arrange for a birthday party, the half-time father will at some time find himself doing all these things.

Developing competence in these daily aspects of parenting is not only a matter of skills and self-confidence, it is also a matter of identity. Men do not measure their own competence by how well they nurture children until they willingly assume parenting tasks. Somehow, in an intact marriage, the couple presents a screen to a small child. Bathroom doors remain closed, as do bedroom doors. In some families it is all right to walk in on Mommy but not on Daddy, or vice versa, perhaps depending on the sex of the child. Often adults protect each other from the child. "Mommy is busy now," or, "you shouldn't go in there when Daddy is resting," etc. This screening becomes more difficult and needs to be more deliberate when there is only one parent. Many fathers have difficulty deciding just how much intimacy they want to encourage. Some men who for the first time are presenting themselves to their children as *real people* feel that the child should have access to them at all times. Perhaps their bedroom door should be open at night, or at least left ajar, so that it is clear that they are home. This generally does not become a problem until the father becomes involved in a sexual relationship. Often men who have their children half the time limit such involvement to times when the child is not there. But in the natural course of events, as other relationships become more intense, some men or their partners feel that there is something unnatural in leaving the children out of it. "I want them to know that I am a sexual being as well," said one father. "I want them to know that sex is a normal part of a close relationship between a man and a woman," said another. Many fathers who have come from marriages where little affection was expressed want to provide a model for their children of more expressiveness and warmth. Some fathers are learning to show their feelings for the first time, initiated partly through their intimacy with the child.

Thus, a whole new set of boundaries has to be established. It is best if the relationship between the father and the child or children has reached some stability before the new person is introduced. In other words, if the father has been able to establish some boundaries between himself and the child, it is easier to extend them to another. Otherwise, a newcomer may be used to separate the father from the demands of the child when he has not been able to contain them on his own. In such instances the child would obviously have good reasons to resent the intrusion into the parent-child relationship. On the other hand, the presence of the child can have a sobering effect on the man who has been acting out his fantasies of singleness. One father's active social life was curtailed after his young daughter walked into his bedroom one Sunday morning, looked down on the woman sleeping next to him and said, *"Which one is that?"* "I don't want them growing up thinking that you can change real relationships daily and they mean nothing," he said, and, in fact, began to work towards developing a deeper relationship with one woman.

Some men have hesitated to bring a new lover into the household, and make sure that the relationship has some possibility of permanence before introducing the children. Since the children had gone through one separation already, there is a concern that any subsequent loss of someone to whom they might become attached could cause the old feelings to reverberate.

The half-time fathers have much leeway in arranging their lifestyles. They can, if they choose, live a very diverse life alternating between responsible parenthood and carefree single-hood on a weekly basis. They can also integrate the two halves of their lives and use the best parts of each to establish continuity and stability in their lives. The first seems to be an early stage of adjustment, and most fathers after a while opt for the latter, more integrated, lifestyle.

EX-SPOUSE

Joint custody—is it for everyone?

In our research we have become impressed by the positive consequences of joint-custody arrangements—the personal growth of the father, and the possibility of having two parents and two homes for the child, thus providing him or her with extra support and care. In fact, the publicity attending joint-custody cases and the popularity of such arrangements have been on the rise. There need to be some special circumstances, however, which make joint custody workable, and it is important that these be considered.

A small number of mavericks or "radicals" in the legal and mental health professions have been recommending joint custody as a means of undoing the blanket lack of consideration for the rights of fathers often evidenced by the courts. This has made joint custody into a pseudo-political issue, and a rallying point for many angry and frustrated fathers who had been unable, for whatever reason, to arrive at a satisfactory solution to their marital conflict either legally or informally.

While we are in sympathy with the rights and needs of disenfranchised fathers, we feel strongly that the half-time arrangements which we have described require special considerations. There may be other ways of ensuring the involvement of each parent, whether or not they have legal custody, which do not entail an actual division of the child's residency. Forcing a child to spend half-time with a parent (mother or father) who is ill suited for daily child care can obviously be as detrimental to the child's well-being as having no contact at all.

One of the major preconditions of a satisfactory joint-custody arrangement is the possibility of developing and maintaining a cooperative relationship between the ex-spouses. As is clear from our narratives of marital breakup, there is usually a great deal of mutual antagonism. No matter how civilized a couple wishes to behave, how reasonable they are about their separation arrangements, how considerate about mutual obligations, there is anger, hurt, and frustration which take time even to admit, and especially to express and dispel.

Cynthia's mother and father had been married for seven years. It was a young marriage. They both were college seniors, but they were not immature. Both seemed to know what they wanted out of life: John was to go to law school; Abby was a psychology major, and was outgoing, energetic and smart. Their courtship and early marriage had all the excitement of two active, independent people with full lives together and on their own. John had admired her spirit and energy, and found her an attentive and helpful kibitzer to his law studies. After graduation, she worked at a job of her own which substantially covered their joint expenses. Their sex life was good as far as they were able to judge, having had little experience with others. Abby seemed happy with John, though he had never been sure whether his apparent adequacy depended on Abby's lack of experience with other men. He suspected, though, that their situation was not atypical, and concluded that they were as happy as anyone he knew.

As John's law practice became a reality and his success seemed to depend on his wholeheartedly throwing himself into his work, he had less time for himself and Abby. In the beginning it seemed purely practical. He had less time, and he had to put his work first because their future financial well-being depended on it. Abby was the understanding wife, and she did not complain about dinners alone. When John was there, he was careful to participate as fully as he could in the cooking and cleaning required to make their lives comfortable.

There had been an unspoken understanding that eventually they would have a family and that John's productivity was an important precondition for making that possible. Since Abby's career was not viewed by them as equally necessary to their future lives together, it did not seem to have the same intensity for her; still, she enjoyed it, was good at it, and was well rewarded.

Working for his family, present and future, fitted John's image of a successful family man. If it took some of the space and energy that had previously contributed to direct intimacy with his wife, he seemed hardly aware of it. At least it was not contrary to his expectations: a man works for his family, and he and they must bear the minor deprivations it may require.

For five days a week John was at his office by eight-thirty; not a breakfast eater, he had his cup of coffee on the run. The first part of the week always seemed more crowded, and he would stay in the office late, making up for the time he "wasted" on the weekend. Although he generally took some work home for the weekend, he rarely managed to get it done and, instead, gave in to the plans that Abby had made for them, or ended up simply spending time with her. He often wished that Abby was more understanding in helping him to be less indulgent, and that she would let him work.

To reduce the conflict between Abby's demands and his perceived need to devote his energy to his work, John became adept at not paying attention to his wife. What he had not understood fully, perhaps, was that Abby was in conflict too: she understood John's pride at being a good lawyer and successful provider, and she was proud of him, but she also saw their relationship slipping. When she tried to draw him nearer to herself she wondered if she was being selfish and overly dependent. It seemed to her that he was less sensitive to her now and that, as a consequence, she had less power in the relationship. Yet she did not want to be one of those wives who needed constant reassurance that they were loved. She had her own career and her own friends. Since John was doing what he was doing for the two of them and for their future family, perhaps this would be a good time to begin to think about starting a family. Perhaps that way she, like John, would be contributing more directly to their joint future. Perhaps that would be a way to recapture some of the intimacy that was being obscured.

John and Abby, at this stage of their marriage, were caught in the traditional expectations of their relative contributions to the family: John, the husband, was busy securing their economic future; Abby, the wife, was concerned with the quality of their present lives. Their child was to bridge the present and the future.

With the birth of Cynthia, Abby's life changed drastically. It was clear now that her life was based at home. Cynthia was an active and a rewarding baby, and both parents were delighted with her. John's reaction, as soon as he was not needed at home was to throw himself even more determinedly into his work. He now had real family obligations. Perhaps they should buy a house? Cynthia would need to go to college. She should have brothers and sisters. Abby tried to show that she was a competent mother who did not need to rely overly on John's help, so she dared not object to his late working hours lest it appeared that, with all her training, ability, and energy, she could not manage the simple tasks of mothering.

It took Abby a whole year to begin to feel dissatisfied with her current situation. She had always been an initiator; it was one of the things John liked about her. She always seemed to know what she wanted and how to go after it. But suddenly Abby's life was totally circumscribed by the needs of others: how long the baby slept, how much work John had, when his clients could see him, and when the well-baby clinic had an opening, all determined her daily schedule. By late evening she was often too tired to take advantage of the child-free time, and just as glad to get some sleep herself while John brought out the papers he had left over from his day.

Abby thought about going back to work but she was still weaning the baby and it seemed impossible to arrange for the kind of time she felt was necessary with her baby, to work, to have time with her husband. When she thought about all the things she would like to do, it seemed as if she would have to be three people at least, with three times the energy she had to summon. She was reluctant to complain, and what was there to complain about? She had a lovely baby she wanted, and a successful husband she loved. Besides, she had an image of herself to maintain as a competent and happy person, the Abby that everyone knew. She already knew the *one* answer to any complaint she might voice. It was: *"Well, what did you expect?"* And indeed, what had she expected? Well, perhaps she had expected to make that image of a family a satisfying reality, but instead it remained only an image; the reality, most of the time, was a once active woman, now tired and confined, occasionally attended by a busy husband.

This was the situation when Cynthia was one year old and John's and Abby's marriage began to go on the rocks. At first the change was very subtle. To John, Abby seemed to be too involved with the baby, but not as happy as he would have expected. He felt neglected by her; she did not respond to him as eagerly as she once had. Still, he knew that she was tired a lot, that the baby was demanding, and he did not want to add his own demands to her burdens. He thought he'd wait it out. She seemed less interested in what had gone on in the office, in news she once listened to happily. He still tried to be interested in everything she had to tell him about the baby and her day, though it was often distracting from what he *had* to think about.

As John became concerned, he talked to a few male friends who had had children, and they assured him that it would pass. It was suggested that they should get sitters more often and try to get out—just the two of them. As far as John understood, he was doing the best he could. His practice flourished, and he was as attentive to Abby as he had time to be. His wife was becoming less interesting to him, and he began to have fantasies about other women, albeit guiltily. Their sex life began to be less satisfying, and he was no longer sure if he remembered correctly that he once thought it was fine. He tried to understand and make allowances, but underneath he was beginning to feel angry. They both had to make sacrifices: he was doing his job well; why couldn't Abby appreciate that and try to do her part with the same commitment?

It is not clear to John to this very day what would have happened to their pattern of dissatisfaction had it not coincided with the women's movement. The women's movement articulated Abby's dissatisfaction and focused her energies which had come adrift through their changed lives. But most importantly, it provided her with people she could talk to, who were jointly developing a response to Abby's unspoken question about expectations. At first, it seemed really good to John that she began to have an interest outside the home. She met with other women and needed an occasional evening away from home. When those occasions turned into regular weekly meetings, John was a little unnerved but he willingly agreed to "babysit" for her. Abby became more and more involved; the weekly evening turned into two afternoons, when she helped write pamphlets and did other activities related to her women's group. In fact, Abby was spending more and more time with other women and, although John didn't always have to babysit since she often took the baby with her, he was being neglected—maybe not as neglected as he thought he was, but still no longer the center of the household.

Abby began to question John's work patterns. If, indeed, it was for the family, she said, then perhaps it was just as important to participate directly in the family's needs. John found himself doing more and more child care. Somehow, he could not counter Abby's ideological arguments. He did love her, and he loved the baby, and it made sense to help in the child care. But the time had to be made up somehow. John's "family time" changed from time spent with his wife and child together to time spent taking care of Cynthia while Abby was away. Their lives seemed to take on a new pattern: either Abby was home with the child and he was at work, or he was "babysitting" and she was gone. Time together, originally demanded by Abby as relief from her mothering, no longer seemed important or desirable. They were in fact going their own ways.

When this pattern emerged it relieved John of some of the guilt he was feeling, though he was barely aware of it, about Abby's confinement in the house. Besides, many of his friends were in similar situations: they had suddenly been made aware of ways they had been oppressing their wives and were eager to make amends. John felt condescending towards his other acquaintances whose lifestyles remained undisturbed by the emerging feminist awareness. He presented himself as a Super Dad. He was still a good lawyer, and yet he now knew all about toilet training and baby food: and he no longer thought that only a mother could comfort a teething baby. Through his new-found pride in fathering he was able to turn the potential accusation of being a "henpecked" husband to a grudging admiration for his all-round competence. He and other young fathers congratulated themselves on how well they did under the new and increasing pressures.

But even this new stance did not reflect in a positive way in his marriage. It was really Abby's appreciation he wanted most: after all, he was doing it for her. But she seemed more and more distant and acted as if he was doing no more than his obligation, and that only under pressure. His new helpfulness was not being rewarded by his wife. Child care became an area of competition instead of cooperation. He was no longer willing to accede to Abby's way of dealing with Cynthia just because she was the mother. He felt he knew his daughter just as well, and perhaps at times was better equipped to deal with her.

While Abby began to question the priority of work for John and his prerogatives associated with being a provider, he began to question her prerogatives in her role as the primary caretaker. The antagonism between them increased. It turned into competition, and it was reflected in their increasingly infrequent and unsatisfactory sex life. The breakup was on the way.

John is typical of those fathers in our sample who had had extensive child-care experience prior to the marital breakup. This is not necessarily a prerequisite for joint custody. Many of the fathers who had a different experience learned child care and homemaking skills after separation. It is, however, more likely that a father who feels able to undertake daily care of a small child will think in terms of sharing that care with his ex-wife. In other words, fathers who ask for and obtain joint custody are more likely to have been involved with the care of children prior to separation.

The events precipitating the breakup are as varied as the couples involved, but in each case a process of readjusting the power of the two partners and the resultant strains of the readjustment can be observed. Some women found new sexual interests, or simply other nonsexual interests—work or study—which reduced their willingness to work out a difficult marriage. Others, with the support of the women's movement, rejected relating to men altogether and tried to make their lives sexually and otherwise exclusively with other women. The men, in turn, frequently looked to extramarital relationships for the emotional rapport missing in the marriage. Perhaps a realization that what had come into question was not mutual affection but the distribution of power in the marriage might have been a useful insight.

For John and Abby the final stress came when Abby decided to take a week-long trip with some women from her group, and asked John to take care of Cynthia for that time. John could not bring himself to say that she must not do it, which was what he wanted to say. He felt powerless and overwhelmed. Once his practical objections, which had to do with work and managing, were overcome, he was not able to object on the true grounds of his feelings. This resulted in a *pseudo-agreement* which increased their sense of estrangement. Abby could not feel truly supported by John because she knew he was not doing this wholeheartedly. Yet, she was willing to make the effort required to draw him out, so she could respond to his true objections. The estrangement provided a certain convenience of independence. Had they been willing to engage in a real struggle, as some couples had, explicitly around issues of power in the relationship, they might have been able to discover new meanings in their marriage and a new basis for mutual affection. Without such a struggle eventual separation was inevitable, because only by leading two socially distinct lives could both their *independence* and their *interdependence* be made explicitly clear. And so, paradoxically, it was only after a separation that John and Abby evolved a pattern of sharing and partnership which had not been possible within their conventionally defined marriage. This is true for many divorced couples.

Postseparation Relationship with Spouse

HOLDING ON AND LETTING GO

The most important fact that emerges most clearly from our study is a joint-custody father's ability to work cooperatively with his ex-spouse for the care of the child. There is a desire on the part of each parent to be involved with child care and to allow the ex-spouse to be involved. They value what they themselves do as parents, and value equally their ex-spouse's right to the children and the children's rights and wishes to maintain a strong relationship with both parents. As we have mentioned before, many of these fathers had, for whatever reasons, already been involved in child care. For some, a specific agreement for shared child care was a precondition of the separation.

This does not mean that the joint-custody couples find themselves in agreement all along the way. There are often many struggles and disagreements, but the intent is to resolve them so as to continue joint parenting. Such conflicts fall into two general categories: the nature of the scheduling agreement—who does what, and when—and the nature of the parents' relationship to each other as ex-marital partners and present co-parents. Often the focus of the major struggle can be summarized as "Who is the real parent?" This is behind the common battle over such things as where the children will spend Christmas, and who can expect to sponsor birthday parties. Important holidays and family events are expected to take place at the home of the "real parent."

The coming Thanksgiving and Christmas holidays the first year of John's and Abby's separation was the scene of an angry interchange both in person and on the phone. Abby wanted to be with Cynthia for Christmas; it had always been *her holiday*, she said. They had baked cookies together and made a candy house. John objected to that appropriation. "Your holiday, bullshit," he retorted, and reminded Abby about her tirades against the consumerism and exploitation of the season.

Again, neither could say what was really on their minds. They were afraid to be alone at Christmastime, afraid to expose themselves to the experience of being without a family. They both recognized it enough to arrive at a solution common to many newly separated couples: they pretended to be a couple for that short time. Abby invited John both for Thanksgiving and for Christmas dinner, and he came, a little stiff and uncomfortable, but grateful. Had either of them been seriously involved with someone else by that time, it would have been more difficult. They would have had either to give up their new partners for the day, thus making clear that their definition of family still involved the old ties, or the joint holiday could not have happened. As it was, this way of spending the holiday was not repeated. The following year, they divided Thanksgiving and Christmas. Cynthia came to John's house, as he was then living with a group, and enjoyed the large Thanksgiving they made all together. Abby took her daughter for Christmas, but not before Cynthia had spent Christmas Eve with her father. They agreed that the following year they would reverse the holidays.

SCHEDULING

The two most common arrangements for shared child care are alternating child care weekly or biweekly, or dividing up the week. The latter prevails when either or both parents' work hours make it possible for them to be available some afternoons but not others, as is the case for those who are teaching, or who can schedule their own work for some evenings. Often difficult schedules are tried until one is reached which seems most convenient to both the parents and the child. Fathers are most likely to include weekends in their part of the schedule, continuing the habits of marriage, only to discover after a while that they need some time to themselves and are forced to rearrange the schedule so that it is more equitable. As in John's case, sometimes the scheduling is arranged so as to minimize contact between the ex-spouses. John could have brought Cynthia back to her mother on Sunday evenings, but he prefered to keep her overnight and take her to school in the morning so that he did not need to have the sense of "returning" her to the other parent. At a later date, particularly if John were to become involved with another woman, he might want those Sunday evenings to himself, and might feel less reluctant to have this brief interaction with his ex-wife.

By the end of the second year of separation, schedules tend to be fairly rigid and inflexible. It does not usually start out this way. As in marriage, cooperation is viewed as flexibility and good will; it is likely that one or the other parent will phone to ask for some special arrangements ("Can you keep her a little longer tonight and give her supper because there is something I want to do?" one might say to the other. Or, conversely, "Please bring the child early because we are going on a trip.") These convenience readjustments implement the inevitable changes that have to do with school, weather, or health. But flexibility can become *unreliability,* and goodwill cannot always be expected on the background of past conflicts. So each request for change is an opportunity for conflict and recrimination. This is especially the case when the reasons are not "legitimate" ones of work or health, but when it looks as if one parent is burdening the other in order to have more time free to spend with a new love or in some other pleasurable pursuit. It is then that old resentments are most likely to flare up. And since ex-spouses can not be expected to account to each other how they spend their time, it becomes clear after a short time that the best situation is one where the schedules remain fixed, and where each parent remains responsible for the time assigned to them, relying on friends or paid help to provide the desired flexibility.

"I am tired of being her babysitter," John said, "but I feel bad since I know that Cynthia would rather be with me than with a sitter." That is the bind. How much is the care for the benefit of the other parent, and how much is it for the child? Here again the issue of boundaries is relevant. In defining his child care as a *service to the ex-spouse,* the father is being pulled into the role of a husband, a role which he has been trying to abandon. The change in the nature of the relationship between the ex-spouses must include giving up the husband parts of the role without giving up being a father. It is not an easy task, since within a marriage these roles are rarely, if ever, articulated separately.

The physical separation of separate living quarters does not instantly end small interdependencies. The wife who is left to take care of the family house is likely to call on her ex-spouse when the sink is stopped up and it is too late to call a plumber. A father may be asked to pick up extra groceries on the way home when he is coming to pick up or return the child, or to come to the mother's assistance for a variety of troubles. The father faced with such a request may be reluctant to comply, and yet it is *his* child who is using the sink and who needs the milk tomorrow morning. Thus it is *his* child who will be affected if the mother's household is not running smoothly. He may also be concerned that, if he refused to help out, the frail cooperative arrangement they have just worked out may be threatened. Many men are only too conscious of how much this shared parenting depends on the goodwill of the ex-wife. All social mores point to her as the "real" parent, and it is he who must prove himself in order to merit this label. Without his wife's approval for his parenting attempts he could easily find himself in a court battle, where the prognosis is poor for a satisfying resolution. So he must carefully weigh his discomfort on being still called upon to perform the duties that once went with his role as husband, against the risk of upsetting his newly developed cooperative parenting.

All the pressure doesn't come from the ex-wife. The end of a marital relationship often has little real clarity for the man. He, too, is tempted to make demands on his ex-wife. In the beginning of separation many men report attempting to initiate sexual contact with the ex-spouse, even amidst anger and recrimination. After all, he was attracted to her once, and there is a familiarity in their interaction which can make him feel less lonely and frustrated. Even if unwilling to continue as sexual partners, many wives are willing and available as knowing and sympathetic listeners. Frequently men have difficulty confiding in others, or admitting weakness, and often the only safe person to talk to is an ex-wife who has been privy to many such instances. Some men turn to their ex-wives for emotional support when other relationships fail them, and are willing to discuss not only their work or personal problem, but even troubles with new lovers. This persistence of ties developed over years of intimacy is a very subtle issue.

Gradually boundaries develop. The man must learn to refuse the husbandly help without feeling as if he were abandoning his child. It is the first step to his independence. The woman must refuse the socio-emotional supports expected of a wife in order to make clear the reduced level of their relationship. What finally remains are rigidly circumscribed rights and obligations *directly related to co-parenting*. This relationship need not be either static or limited. It grows and changes with the development of the parents' lives and the changing needs of the growing children. At every stage of the way, new ways of doing things arise, new facets of the relationship are negotiated.

What Is Necessary for Co-Parenting?

The father needs to see himself as sensitive and competent. Both parents will come to understand the advantage to the child of having two parents, even if there are differences that must be overcome. Each parent must begin to trust the other to act in the best interests of the child, and to give them full responsibility for what happens in their house. Each must both take control and relinquish it. Control comes partly through information; both parents want to be fully informed about the child, whether he or she is with them or not, and yet they have to allow privacy and initiative to the other parent.

As we have mentioned before, the joint-custody fathers generally pay less child support to their ex-wives. The fathers may cover some of the major expenses for the children, such as health care and school fees, but these are paid directly to the services involved and not to the mother. Rent, food, and entertainment are large expense categories mentioned by the fathers. The fact that little money is exchanged between the ex-spouses removes one of the major sources of conflict common among divorced couples. It is often easier for an ex-wife to be sympathetic to the father of her children when he is struggling to meet his obligations by cooking and cleaning and juggling work hours (something she herself has experienced and appreciates) than if he puts the same amount of energy into making money to meet the increased child care payments. When the input of the two parents is of the same kind, the possibility of empathy—hence of good will and cooperation—is greatly enhanced. The same is true from the point of view of the children. Most children, if consulted, would probably be glad to see fewer toys and have Daddy put them to bed than try to appreciate the explanation that their father's extended absence is "for them" and that they should be grateful for the brand-new toy which was earned by that deprivation.

CLOSENESS TO CHILDREN

Most fathers whom we have interviewed say that they are closer to their children now than they were during the marriage. When asked why he felt that way, one father of a seven-year-old boy said:

Because now he does not have someone else to turn to; and I do not have someone else to lean on. We can't avoid the hard parts any more. I'm still not as close as I would like to be, but that is a function of my personality.

A father of three children aged eleven, ten, and seven said:

I don't take their continued presence for granted, and I think they sense this. I spend more time with them now.

Closeness takes time to develop. The skills of dealing with children emotionally and expressively have to be learned. There are stages in these developments. The first stage we have called the time of "doing." This must be familiar to any father: the first panic of being faced with spending two or three whole days with a small child is often handled by a frantic perusal of local newspapers for any "event" which will help fill up their parenting hours. The circus, zoos, museums, restaurants, and children's shows are well attended by dutiful fathers, who, slightly bored and self-consciously patient, are fulfilling their parenting obligations.

"I thought I had to be with them every moment of the time,"

said one weekend father, "and provide all the entertainment and make sure they were happy and interested all the time."

Fathers who have their children half-time or full-time cannot put such a heavy burden on themselves and are, therefore, forced to integrate their own activities and the outside activities of their children into a coherent lifestyle.

When John learned to expect Cynthia to amuse herself with whatever was available to her while he prepared dinner, he had learned to *be* with her instead of *doing* things with her. This is the second stage of single parenting—when the father has learned how to *be* with the child without the constant distraction, and perhaps emotional distancing, of organized activities. The father ceases to be solely the entertainer, keeping busy or even bribing the children with objects and activities. Life becomes normalized and routinized. Trips to the laundry or the bank are something to be done together. These daily routines are an opportunity for the child to participate in the realities of the father's life, and they shift the burden of activities from the child's interests—i.e., what movie, etc., the child might like—to the real survival needs of this family unit. Such a shift reasserts the proper balance of authority. It is the father who is again in charge, who defines the needs of the unit, and who responds to them.

When a father is no longer indulgent out of insecurity, guilt or a lack of firm definition of parenting behavior, the child loses the inappropriate centrality in the relationship. Relieved of that responsibility, he or she is able to grow in independence and autonomy and to develop an appropriate sense of expectations about the father. The father is able to put his commitment to the child into perspective. He knows his relationship to his child is important, but he also knows that he has other interests and commitments. He no longer needs to perceive the child as overly demanding or needful. It is up to him to decide which demands are to be honored and which can be ignored. He can begin to develop a real, lasting and mutually interdependent relationship with his children, which is not oppressive to either parent or child and which will change and grow with the changing needs of both.

CHAPTER 5

A Man and His Ex-Wife

Almost all heterosexual adults in our society anticipate two major events in their lives: marriage and parenthood, often in quick succession of each other and usually in that order. Recently we were discussing marriage with a young man of twenty-one. Contrary to current statistics, he was planning to marry young. "Why?" we asked. "So that I can have children early because I would like them to be half grown by the time I get a divorce. That way it will be easier for me to take care of them." This is a seemingly rational life plan for someone who, himself a child of divorce, accepts it as yet another inevitable event.

What this kind of expectation will do to the consciousness surrounding the divorce process is difficult to foretell. It is clear from the interviews we have conducted and from the experience of therapists and social workers that divorce is a painful, disruptive event for most young and middle-age adults. It is an undoing: "dissolving the marriage contract," "putting aside the spouse," says the dictionary. But, in fact, it is also dissolving and putting aside so many parts of oneself—feelings, habits, attachments and daily routines—that it is often difficult to even imagine a self and a life without the structure of the marriage or the company of the particular spouse.

The legal aspects of the marital breakup bring to the intimate life of the family all the terminology of criminal proceedings: there is a plaintiff and a defendant; there are charges and counter-charges; guilt is admitted or denied. The hurts of the relationship are labeled, made public, reaffirmed, and often exaggerated for the sake of a clear court case. In spite of the increasing attempts to make "no-fault" divorce the norm, it is still likely to be in the lawyer's office that the husband or the wife becomes fully aware of the extent to which they have been, or are about to be, "done in."

Prior to the divorce, the married parents share four major areas of their lives: personal intimacy, social life, economic cooperation and parenting responsibility. The particular arrangements of these functions, who does what and how it is done, differ widely from family to family. A divorce disrupts all of them, but the extent of the disruption differs from couple to couple, depending on the priorities they gave to those marital arrangements. In other words, the divorce relationship depends to a large extent on what marriage had meant to the couple in the first place. This makes it as difficult to generalize about relationships between ex-spouses as it is to generalize about marriages. We found couples who continue to work together, or even share a house after "separation," comfortable in their new platonic friendship, and others who limit their contact to an occasional date but seem unable to completely forego the habit of sexual intimacy. Older relatives, aunts, uncles and in-laws often view such behavior with the same disapproval that once was reserved for pre-marital goings on.

In contrast to the private and wide-ranging lifestyles within marriage, the divorce dispositions are public and uniform. The law assumes, for the most part, that women are most likely to stay home and take care of children and that fathers are the appropriate breadwinners. Aside from property disposition, most divorce agreements spell out the financial obligations of the father and provide for some limited access to the children through regular visitation.

Currently there have been numerous changes in the roles of men and women. Many couples are working out their own individual arrangements, both in marriage and after, as to who takes on what responsibility. In older marriages, where the wife has spent many years as a homemaker, there is probably little likelihood of equalizing the economic potential of the two parents. In such cases, the courts need to ensure that the mother and children are not left destitute. But, for many younger couples, an equality both of economic support and of emotional investment in the children is approaching reality. Because of these recent changes in lifestyle expectations, the conventional assumptions behind divorce laws are rapidly becoming inappropriate for an increasing segment of young couples.

It is because of the changing social status of men and women that much of the sociological material concerning both the preconditions and the effects of divorce soon becomes outdated. A major study of divorce (Goode, 1956) formulated and tested the following hypotheses: (1) divorce is traumatic; (2) wives experience divorce in terms of guilt and punishment; (3) divorce has adverse consequences on children; (4) continued contact between the ex-spouses creates antagonism between them or maintains the attachment, both outcomes viewed as undesirable. Although the hypotheses were not completely supported by the data, their formulation alone tells us much about the common assumptions of the *"shoulds"* of postdivorce relationships.

These are the same assumptions which underlie the argument presented in *Beyond the Best Interests of the Child* (1973), and they have been widely used by lawyers and judges to support their custody decisions. The book takes as a given that the divorcing parents are in irresolvable conflict with each other, and the authors strongly discourage any co-parenting arrangement. They consider such arrangements as impossible to negotiate and as potentially disruptive to the child, since they are bound to engender "severe and crippling loyalty conflicts" (p. 13). This has been widely quoted as a justification for disenfranchising one parent (usually the father) in custody decisions.

In the last ten years, however, while divorce rates have increased rapidly, conditions attending divorce have changed in the following ways:

1. In some segments of society, the social stigma attached to divorced adults and children of divorce has decreased markedly. This reduces the need to blame the divorce on the "other" partner.
2. Increased social approval of personal decisions based on need for individual fulfillment and growth has provided an ideology which allows a quick recovery from feelings of guilt and inadequacy when the marriage fails. The reduced concern with guilt and blame, both self-assumed and defensively projected, reduces some of the trauma associated with divorce. The introduction of no-fault divorce has given social recognition to this new attitude.
3. Increased possibility of economic independence for women makes breaking up a marriage less of an economic disaster for both partners.
4. Increased prevalence of divorced families makes it possible to create self-help networks and to develop norms, models, and awareness for reinforcing new identities and new lifestyles after divorce.
5. And finally, the general increase in acceptance of cultural diversity has allowed the emergence of different family forms. We no longer view the "father-mother-and-children" family as the only viable form. New single-parent homes as well as multi-generation families, or step families, are seen as positive environments for child-rearing.

These changes, as well as the lowered age and increased educational level of divorcing couples, have significantly reduced the most conflict-ridden and trauma-producing conditions attending divorce. Amicable divorce, once an anomaly, is increasingly becoming the expectation, as is co-parenting after separation.

And the courts, albeit often reluctantly, have been forced to recognize these changes, and are making it easier for both parents to remain connected to the children.

Other studies of postdivorce families (Stack, 1976; Walker, Rogers and Messinger, 1977; Brown, Feldberg, Fox and Kohn,

1976), as well as our own, indicate that the ex-spouse remains the most important and commonly utilized resource for child-care assistance. Divorced parents who can avail themselves of emotional, financial and practical help from the children's other parent are clearly in a better position than those who must parent alone, or worry about having to impose their children on nonrelated adults, or pay for services. Relatives are rarely available to help with the children. Not only do grandparents usually live far away, but grandmothers now are likely to be employed. This is true for both middle-class and working-class families. The nuclear family has been a very isolated unit indeed, and any further division of this unit leaves the solitary adult greatly overburdened.

For fathers who take on a large share of child care, the ex-spouse is not only an important practical resource but also a source of approval and encouragement for their parenting behavior. Mothers who tell their children that they think well of what their father does with them can have an important effect on stabilizing the father-child bond. Many men are acutely aware of their wives' approval and disapproval, and are grateful for the support they are given as parents. Children, too, seeing their father in a new role and a new setting, can be reassured and helped to accept the changes by a positive attitude from their mother.

Thus there is much to gain by both parties in maintaining a cooperative parenting arrangement. The father who sees his children weekly is not likely to resent his support payments or to default on his other obligations: it does not require a court action to remind him of his children's needs. A mother who finds her ex-husband genuinely involved and concerned about the chil-dren, putting time and energy into this relationship, is better able to set aside the resentments of the broken marriage and view him in a more sympathetic light. Common concerns, combined with the possibility of having partial relief from the children by someone who shares equally the concern for their well being, is quickly seen by many divorced couples as an advantage worth maintaining, no matter how much one wishes it were possible to totally put the other spouse out of one's life.

Developing such cooperation, as rational as it may sound, is by no means an easy task. "Few events in the life cycle require more extensive change in activities, responsibilities and living habits (or cause greater alteration of outlook on life) than does the change from one marital status to another" (Bogue, 1949). While anger, resentment and blame can be useful to mobilize energy necessary to achieve an emotional distance from the marriage and ex-spouse, they must be experienced, released and finally put aside, if the couple wishes to develop a cooperative parenting relationship. Eventually, both emotional distance from the ex-partner and cooperation must develop, through separating the father and the husband roles. The development of an independent relationship with the children is the first step in separating these roles and in regaining, outside of marriage, some of the lost parts of oneself.

"I was once close to my wife; I felt loved and responsibility. Now I have these feelings towards my children, and they provide me with that kind of closeness," said one of the fathers.

"In all the changes and shifting in the beginning of separation, they [the children] were like my lifeline while I was sinking in the pain of loss and fear," said another.

Separation to Cooperation

The process of emotional separation is often obscured by such practical matters as dividing property and agreeing on alimony amounts. The person who insists on having the family silver may really be saying that they are the one who loved more, gave more, or put more meaning into the marriage. Financial accountings take the place of needed emotional accounting. How effectively and how quickly they can be accomplished differ with each marriage and the events which led to its ending.

For some couples the pattern of indifference and separatedness had already set much before the decision to take separate residences was made. Such couples may already have worked through many of their feelings about each other, and now, going their own way may seem the natural next stage in their lives. For these couples, the emotional accounts were settled before the breakup. Often, as in the case of John and Abby, even the pattern of separate parenting had been established. But this is true only of a small proportion of divorcing parents. The majority separates because of conflict, and the separation is often viewed as a tentative arrangement designed to relieve unbearable tension. At such a crisis time it is difficult to anticipate all the implications of the breakup. Thus, no matter how long such a decision may have been in the making, many individuals find themselves "suddenly" in a situation for which they feel totally unprepared.

The majority of the men in our sample reported feeling closer to their children now than they did before separation and ascribed this feeling to time spent as sole caretakers. In short, the bond between father and child is important not only as an emotional attachment in its own right, but also as a connection with the past family life and as a continuing tie that provides stability and direction for the future. It also serves as an emotional anchor for attaching the positive feelings which persist about the marriage and about the ex-spouse, but which otherwise stand in the way of personal emotional separation. It is not uncommon for respondents to describe their wives in most negative terms but to add with a certain pride, "she's a wonderful mother." This evaluation also makes it feasible for the father to continue some of the marital dependency on his ex-wife's opinions and judgments where the children are concerned, and yet to cease being emotionally involved with her.

The whole issue of continued interdependency between divorced parents has received little support or attention in sociological literature. Dependency between ex-spouses has been viewed in negative terms only, either as the problem of continued economic dependence of the wife (Brown, Feldberg, Fox and Kohn 1976; Walker, Rogers and Messinger, 1973), or as a problem of the "persistence of attachment" (Fisher, 1973, Weiss, 1976) which prevents divorced couples from making new lives for themselves.

In the course of this study, our attention has been drawn to the way continued support, both emotional and economic, between divorced parents becomes a structured part of new postdivorce family arrangements, and an important consideration in planning new careers, new lifestyles and even remarriage. This support does not need to bind the couple to the past marriage, but can provide a base from which to venture into new relationships.

Whether the ex-spouses remain available to each other for anything from emotional support to house repair must be worked out item by item. Sometimes the desire to prove to the ex-spouse that, in spite of everything that has happened he is a "good guy" will make an estranged husband, albeit reluctantly, drop everything to drive his ex-wife to a dentist appointment or meet her to discuss a work problem with which he had been helpful in the past.

One divorced mother confided that she is much more likely to turn to her ex-husband for help than her current lover, for two reasons; first, she wants to make the point that she is still a family member and has the right to make demands, and second, she feels that her ex-husband will not need to be repaid for his help, while with anyone else she is incurring an obligation.

It is important, however, to understand that certain boundaries must be established and that clarity about these boundaries will stabilize the postdivorce relationship. The difference between cooperation in a marriage and co-parenting after separation is as follows: in an ongoing relationship the partners hope that by anticipating and fulfilling each other's needs they will deepen the relationship and increase their sensitivity and openness to each other. The postdivorce cooperation, on the other hand, has a more contractual character. What can and cannot be expected must be spelled out clearly, since the intent is to maintain the relationship within specified bounds and not to allow it to increase beyond these bounds. Although a refusal to accede to the demands of the other partner may risk intensifying the conflict, in the long run it stabilizes the relationship. Understanding the importance of adhering to the co-parenting contract will release the partners from feelings of guilt about not being more available to each other. As long as the original agreement was carefully arrived at and justified by the needs of the children, a somewhat rigid adherence to that agreement creates a climate of trust and predictability which is imperative for cooperative parenting.

Patterns of Postseparation Relationships

For most couples, successful separation of the co-parenting relationship from the intimacy of a love relationship requires a degree of emotional independence which takes time and personal growth to achieve. This is not always possible. Thus the following patterns of postdivorce relationships emerge:

1. Men who have successfully been able to effect a comfortable but distant relationship with their ex-spouse and to remain cooperative and interdependent as co-parents,
2. Men who remain in an unsorted limbo of familial ties, still very tied to their ex-spouse, reliving old conflicts in a volatile and emotionally charged relationship of love and hate, and finally
3. Men who avoid contact with their ex-spouse to minimize the emotional pull which continues to affect them strongly, or to defend themselves against the demand for involvement which comes from their ex-wives.

In order to gauge the extent and intensity of the still existing relationship with the ex-wife, we asked the men in our sample the following set of questions: How would you characterize your present relationship with your ex-wife? (Table 1) At present, how often do you communicate with her? (Table 2) Which one of you is most likely to initiate contact? (Table 3) How do you rate your ex-wife as a parent? (Table 4) What are the three major characteristics that best describe your ex-wife? What is your most common emotion when communicating with your ex-spouse? (Table 5) We asked a group of questions about the content of their communication. The data was analyzed for the frequency, intensity and quality of contact with the ex-spouse.

On the basis of that analysis we evaluated the type of relationship that fathers in each custody group were most likely to have with their ex-wives.

COOPERATIVE BUT DISTANT—TYPE I

The fathers who shared child care half-time appear to exemplify the successful sorting out of the parent-husband relationship. These men are most likely to characterize their relationship with their ex-wife as *distant* (55 percent) or *friendly* (21 percent), and although they are in touch with their wives several times a week, or even daily (17 percent), they are least likely of all the groups to see themselves as the sole initiators of that contact and most likely to say that both parents are equally likely to call. In spite of this frequent contact, and in spite of the fact, that of all the fathers, they are most likely to live within a short distance of their ex-wives (83 percent live no more than a half-hour's time away), the half-time fathers are the least likely of all the part-time fathers to meet socially with their ex-spouse (62 percent say "never"—see Table 6), and least likely to view her as an intimate (69 percent say that they do not discuss any personal problems with their ex-wives—see Table 7).

However, when asked about the ex-wife's abilities as a parent, 93 percent refer to her as a "good" or "excellent" mother; only one father in that group considers his wife an "inadequate" mother, and one other merely "adequate." When asked to describe their ex-wives, the latter two half-time fathers were the only men in that group to give a negative description as their *first response*. All the other joint-custody fathers gave either neutral or positive attributes mainly in the area of personal maturity, with responses such as "mature," "responsible," "caring," "unselfish," "good mother," etc. Negative *first* responses were given by over one-half of the occasional fathers (57 percent) and full-time fathers (52 percent). Full-time fathers were least likely to describe their wives as mature or responsible, and the occasional fathers were least likely to give positive responses in the relational category. Note that this does not mean that half-time fathers had nothing but good things to say about their ex-wives. Over one-third gave negative descriptions as their *second* and *third* responses.

We understand this to be an indication that for those men who had been able to sort out the separate aspects of their relationship, the immediate response to the ex-partner is based on the evaluation of her as a parent. Others, less involved in parenting, are still considering their wives in terms of the failed personal intimacy—that is, they consider their ex-wives to be adequate parents and yet describe them in overwhelmingly negative terms.

When asked if their wives spoke well of *their* parenting efforts, 72 percent of the half-time fathers answered "often," followed by 65 percent of quarter-time fathers. This answer was reported by only 35 percent of the weekend-only fathers, and even fewer full-time fathers (26 percent). The weekend-only fathers had the highest proportion of men saying that their ex-wife "never" said anything good about them to the children (48 percent), followed by almost half of the full-time fathers (44 percent). It seems, then, that as the amount of shared child rearing increases, so does the mutual support and respect that the ex-spouses give to each other as parents.

Different child-care schedules require different degrees of cooperation between the partners. The widespread expression of insecurity and self-doubt concerning parenting which are common to newly separated men indicate that most men view their wives as being the competent parents. The woman is seen as understanding what the children need, either naturally or through continuing contact with the children, and is expected to direct and instruct the father in his interaction with the children. This view that the mother is the most appropriate parent is also held and reinforced by the courts, and often hinders divorced men from developing a separate relationship with his children, independent of the approval and orchestration of the wife.

The practical reality of the legal power of the mother as the custodial parent must also not be overlooked. In our sample, only slightly over one-half of the men were divorced (57 percent). The remainder were separated from their wives, for the most part informally (32 percent). These figures are similar across the different child care groups. The visiting father is most likely to be formally divorced (64 percent). When the separation is informal, the child-care arrangements have no legal standing. Even among the fathers who have their children full-time, only 54 percent had made those arrangements through the legal system. Among the half-time fathers, only one-third (34 percent) had legal joint-custody arrangements. For the quarter-time fathers and the weekend fathers the numbers of men whose visiting schedules were legally established were even smaller (16 percent and 25 percent respectively).

The maintenance of the informal child-care schedule depends on the good will of the parents. Since in most cases the wives have legal custody, they have the power to revoke these arrangements. The insecurity evoked by this tends to be intensified by a feeling which many men shared that the mother, or indeed any female person, may be preferred by the children to the father. This insecurity is particularly characteristic of the fathers who did not participate much in child care prior to the separation. They know little about their children and often feel that the children regard them as near strangers. It is not surprising then, that when we asked for the "major emotion" which characterizes their dealings with the ex-spouse, *"anger"* and *"mistrust"* were the two responses most commonly mentioned by both the half-time and the full-time fathers. This posture of defensive watchfulness is most evident early in the separation, before the stability of the parenting arrangements has been tested through time.

THE UNSORTED HUSBAND-FATHER—TYPE 2

In contrast to the half-time fathers, quarter-time fathers present a picture of conflict and confusion vis-à-vis their ex-spouses. Their parental roles and participation in the children's life are not clearly defined and tend to be more determined by the ex-wives. The men we interviewed were categorized as "quarter-time fathers" if they spent no less than seven, or more than fourteen days a month with their children. These men who approached the upper limits of that time were spending almost as much time in child care as the men who considered themselves to be sharing the parenting equally with their wives. Yet their self-definition as parents was much different, as was the relationship with their ex-wives.

"Frustration" was the most frequent response given by this group to describe their feelings about the ex-spouse. Forty-three percent of the respondents mentioned this, as opposed to only 25 percent of the less participating fathers. "Frustration" was mentioned by only two of the joint-care fathers, and four of the full-time fathers.

The sense of low control is further underscored by the finding that these are the men most likely to rate their present child-care arrangements as "unsatisfactory" and to report the highest degree of conflict with their ex-wives on child-rearing issues. At the same time they are more likely than men in the other groups to go to their wives or ex-wives for child-rearing advice. They also report "discussion" and "accepting of differences" as the most common ways of resolving marital conflict. We can only assume that these conciliatory attitudes are an expression of the sense of ineffectiveness about parenting input.

This group of men is most likely to continue to meet their wives socially, or to contact them "simply to keep in touch"; this is different from fathers in the other groups who limit their reasons for contact with their ex-wives to issues of parenting and child-rearing problems. They are likely to report spending holidays with their ex-wives as a way of being in the company of their children. Two-thirds of the fathers in this group reported such family get-togethers, in contrast to less than a half of each of the other groups.

Furthermore, these fathers, more than ones from any other group reported that their relationship with the ex-wife was "friendly" or "very friendly"; yet, like the weekend fathers, they reported a great deal of conflict both over their wives' child-rearing styles and the women's own lifestyles. In spite of the high degree of discord, they are the most likely of all the fathers to communicate with their wives daily or several times a week (81 percent) and least likely to let more than a week elapse with no contact. More than half say that they are the ones who initiate the contact (57 percent), while only a third of the half-time fathers, and a fourth of each of the other groups, are the initiators of contact. (The relationship between initiation of contact and control of child-care information can be inferred from the finding that joint-care fathers see contact as mutual, whereas full-custody fathers are most likely to be contacted by their ex-wives.) More than half the men in this group say that "ideally" they would prefer to have the children full-time but cannot imagine being able to do so without such major changes in their lives as remarriage or change of residence or career. Thirty percent say that they would like to take care of their children half-time, but not necessarily through a formal joint custody arrangement.

Although many of the fathers in this group spend as much time with their children as the joint-custody fathers, they do not define themselves as co-parents and consequently pay larger alimony and child-support payments than the joint–custody fathers we interviewed. Their attachment to their families can also be seen in the fact that they tend to live closer to the ex-wife and communicate with her more often than men from any of the other groups. Even though they report a great deal of unresolved conflict with the ex-spouses, rather than avoiding contact they seem to seek them out for discussion and argument. The discussions range over many areas of their lives, and are not limited to child-care issues. The men are likely to ask their wives' advice on everything from their careers to their social life. Yet, they do not report their ex-wives as being especially helpful, and often find the discussions conflict-inducing.

Considering the high amount of discussion, the degree of conflict and the many mixed emotions expressed toward the ex-wives, we conclude that this is a group of men who have been unable to develop, or who are still in the process of developing, clear boundaries between their roles as husbands and their roles as fathers. Since their lives appear to be still involved with the lives of their ex-wives, it is difficult to assess their motivation for parenting. It may be that taking on child care is a way to stay close to the children's mother, or, conversely, it may be that as long as these men do not define themselves as autonomous and legitimate parents they view their continued involvement with their ex-wives as necessary to the maintenance of close contact with the children.

It may very well be that the high degree of conflict with the ex-wife reported by this group of men is the response of the ex-spouse to the lack of clarity in the relationship. In other words, the women may be responding defensively to the attempts at contact and the continued interdependency. Perhaps through this conflict and struggle new adjustments will be made and new boundaries forged which will help these couples to understand how to sort out aspects of their relationships which must be maintained for the sake of co-parenting from those which must be abandoned with the marriage.

WHEN CO-PARENTING FAILS—TYPE 3

The third group of men we have identified are those who find the conflict of the marriage too great, or too painful, even to begin to sort out aspects of cooperative parenting from the chaos of the marital relationship. Most such men remove themselves, sooner or later, from the lives of their ex-wives and children and thus are not in our sample, but they are amply represented in the great numbers of disappearing husbands. Men who appear to fit this description can be also found among the fathers who maintain the minimum amount of contact with their children, as well as those who take over their custody altogether, and solve the conflict by removing the necessity of relating to their ex-wives.

With this in mind, the group of full-time fathers in the sample requires special attention. Despite the fact that these men take care of their children full-time, not all have legal custody of the children. Some of the men arrived at this arrangement with their ex-wives prior to divorce, others were still struggling over custody issues, and still others found themselves "stuck" with the children due to the inability or unwillingness of the mother to care for them. The split between the men who refer to their ex-wife as an "inadequate" mother (55 percent) and those who do not reflects some of these facts. In the former group we find fathers who have become the only parent by default and are still quite angry about it, as well as those who had to prove their wife unfit to gain custody. The remainder have settled, quite amicably, the issue of the children's residence. This latter group depends on their wives for child care and, sometimes, financial assistance, and in general reports a low degree of conflict and disagreement. The former group of full-time fathers reports very little contact with their ex-wives. A large proportion (44 percent) reported that their ex-wives "never said anything good about [them] to the children." Only 10 percent of the fathers in the other groups gave that response. These are the men who, willingly or not, are in control of their children's lives. They report that it is their ex-wives who initiate contact, which they themselves attempt to keep to a minimum. This group, more than any other, mentions "anger" as the main emotion towards their ex-wives. For some of these men, the anger stems from experience with a negative interference on the part of the children's mother in the father's parenting, while other men express anger over the low involvement of their ex-wives with the children, and the futility of their attempts to get more assistance for their parenting efforts. These men often identify strongly with their children, and their anger is prompted by the children's hurt of being abandoned by their mothers.

Similarly, some of the fathers in our weekends-only, or less-than-quarter-time group belong in this last category. These are the men who would like more child care but are prevented from it either by an unwillingness on the part of their ex-wives to grant them extensive parental rights or by their own sense of inadequacy or insecurity as parents. In striking contrast to the other men in our sample, these fathers are most likely to say that their ex-wives encourage the children to seek father substitutes (46 percent) and say bad things about them to the children (48 percent). (Only a negligible number of other part-time fathers and less than a fourth of the full-time fathers report this.) Fathers in this group are also more likely than other men to use courts and professional help to settle disagreements.

It is also possible that some of these men have just the amount of contact with their children that they wish, or perhaps even more than they would like—that is, fathers who see their children every other weekend or less (once a month was the minimum criterion for inclusion in the sample), may do so only as a way of minimally fulfilling their parental obligation. We conclude this from the findings that men in this group are more likely to say that they want less discussion of child-related matters with their ex-wives, rather than more, as is the case with many of the other part-time fathers.

Given the high degree of conflict with the ex-spouse expressed by the men in this group, and the high degree of dissatisfaction with their own lives, we conclude that these are men whose lives as separated fathers have not gone well. They either have not been able to struggle in order to achieve a more satisfactory arrangement or do not see such an arrangement as possible for themselves. These men live further away from their ex-wives than other part-time fathers (often an hour by car), and they report the highest income and the highest level of child-support and alimony payments. They also express the most conflict over money matters. The age, personality and sex-role attitudes of men in that group make them more representative of the conventional visiting divorced father.

Effects of Attitudes Towards the Ex-Wife

When we asked the fathers how good their ex-wives were at handling the children, some interesting differences appeared. Almost all of the quarter-time fathers said their wives were good at handling children, making it appear that these men, whose own involvement was extensive but not clearly defined, may be reluctant to assert themselves vis-à-vis the accepted competence of the mothers. Over three-quarters of the joint-custody fathers viewed their wives as good with children. On the other hand, less than half of both the occasional visitors and the full-time fathers saw their wives as competent. Thus it appears that the men who are least happy with the way their ex-spouses rear the children either feel themselves powerless to affect the situation and handle it by remaining at a distance, or they take over the care of the children altogether.

In other words, the decision about scheduling of child care is related to the attitudes towards the child-rearing skills of the mother. The more the parents are in accord about the child-rearing styles and approve of each other as parents, the more likely they are to cooperatively share the parenting function. The less one parent approves of the competence of the other, the less likely they are to attempt to co-parent, and one or the other parent will assume control of child rearing.

To summarize, divorce leaves men with a range of impressions concerning their ex-spouses. Postseparation parenting depends to a large extent on the opinions of the spouses of each other as *parents*. The more the marital role can be separated from the parenting role, the more the individuals can view each other objectively as to their parenting competence. Some men describe their ex-wives as "beautiful, intelligent and kind"; others as "selfish, neurotic and disgusting" yet, whatever the descriptions, many find it possible to be supportive to each other as parents and to appreciate their mutual relationship with the children despite individual differences. Once a positive judgment of the other spouse as a parent is made, it is possible to develop a cooperative relationship around parenting issues even while there may remain a great deal of distance, or even anger, about more personal issues between the couple. Couples who are able to develop a core of co-parenting can begin to attach the remaining good feelings about each other to that aspect of their relationship while discounting the issues which evoke conflict.

For example, almost all the joint-care father's contact with the ex-wife is around child-care issues; he finds his spouse helpful, available and supportive, but he also expresses many negative feelings about her as a person. The emotional boundaries he has created, which keep him from discussing personal problems or having social contact with his ex-spouse, help to maintain the stability of the co-parenting relationship. Men who have not worked out these boundaries clearly may attempt to use the positive parenting interaction in an attempt to rebuild other disrupted parts of their marital relationship. In such a case, they find themselves in a frustrating situation in which many of their marital conflicts are replayed. Often neither the parenting relationship nor the intimate one becomes resolved.

Role of the Ex-Wife in Fathering

Since the mother continues to be viewed by the legal system as the more appropriate custodial parent, many men are dependent on the good will of their ex-spouses in sharing their control over the children's fate. In many states the non-custodial parent can be refused access to the child's school or medical records, and the concerned father needs his wife's permission to attend a teacher's conference or participate in medical decisions affecting his child. Although most such legalities are not widely reinforced, they nevertheless make the man easily aware of the vulnerability of his position vis-à-vis the child. Even a father whose visiting rights and privileges have been legally spelled out may find them revoked when an ex-spouse finds herself inconvenienced by them. (This is, of course, not to ignore countless women who wish that their ex-husbands would express more interest or spend more time with their children.)

For men who co-parent, relationships with ex-wives also figure prominently in their social life. It is not uncommon for the ex-wife to make it a condition that no other woman may be present when the father takes the children. Such prohibitions usually arise from some preseparation crisis and, under a guise of protecting the children, may be a way of punishing a previously errant husband. Such explicit prohibitions, as well as simply the fear that many men have that their wives will ask the children questions about their personal lives, are serious limitations on the father's freedom with his children. Usually where such a situation exists it becomes attenuated with time. The partners come to care less about each other's lives, the children become uninterested in being used by the adults, and everyone becomes more comfortable with the new lifestyle.

When a new partner does enter the father's life, he may again be concerned that this does not upset the delicate truce he has achieved with the children's mother. At first, the new lover may be kept away from the children so they have little information about her. Later her role may continue to be carefully circumscribed so that the mother does not get the impression that he has passed the care of the children on to someone else. The father may feel disloyal in front of the children by showing affection to someone other than their mother, or unwilling to deal with the feelings of jealousy or rejection which it might evoke in them.

Eventually, as the new relationship deepens and stabilizes, the father and his new partner will have to decide exactly what her role is to be vis-à-vis his whole family. The man now finds himself an intermediary between two family systems. He, his children and the children's mother still form one kind of family unit. He, his children and his new partner are another. Any changes in one affect the other; each must be adjusted to redress the balance.

The men we spoke to reported frequent disagreements with their lovers on matters involving the ex-wife. Financial and custody arrangements of the parents, whether legal or informal, take precedence in the father's household. The new partner, often still insecure in her relationship with the children, feels powerless to affect agreements between the former spouses, at the same time as such agreements determine many of the details of her daily life. The father, caught between, is very likely to collaborate with his ex-spouse in disallowing a legitimate role for the new partner in these negotiations. There are many reasons for this. Often he does not wish his new lover to see certain aspects of himself which may be evident in his dealing with his ex-wife—the old parts of himself. Often, the man is not as assertive against the ex-spouse as he describes, nor is she as much of an ogre as he has made her out to be. Many times he simply doesn't want to "rock the boat," unsure of what his wife's reactions will be. Sometimes the man will have very mixed feelings when the two women do get along and are able to agree among themselves, because he wishes his lover to join him as the ex-wife's adversary. Still others simply feel guilty about having someone new, especially if their ex-wives have not found new partners.

Most of the time, these concerns are well founded. Many wives resist the participation of a new partner in decisions affecting the children. The father is likely to feel responsible for satisfying the desires of both women: "I realized that realistically my wife and Joan just don't get along, and that I have to act as the middleman and keep them away from each other. I don't say to one of them that the other wants or needs something; although that might be fair, they simply won't hear it." Another father described a similar problem: "Alice refuses to recognize that Nancy is really in the kids' lives. Nancy really resents being treated as though she does not exist."

If the new relationship is a serious one which will lead to remarriage, confrontation is almost inevitable. Eventually, a new pattern of interaction which includes the input of both women becomes the mode. How it works out depends greatly on the personalities and particular circumstances of all the adults involved. As time passes and the new partner becomes secure in her family life, while the mother is no longer concerned that her children's affection might be usurped, it is possible for the two women to become united in their common concern for the children, as was the case with the separated parents.

In the end it is the relationship with the children that defines for each of the adults their place in this new postdivorce family. One of the fathers in our sample has written to us recently to say that he had been forced to relocate and forego the joint-custody arrangement he had had for two years. The woman who shared his house for those two years, however, has stayed behind. She not only continues in a close relationship with the children but has become a good friend of the children's mother and provides her with much assistance and support in child rearing.

CHAPTER 6

Making a New Life: Changing Patterns of Work and Intimacy for Fathers without Partners

The raising of children brings pleasure as well as burdens. Child care can be an occasion for growth and development of the parent, as we have described in Chapter 3, and it can also be confining and demanding. There is no question that a family life requires planning and scheduling. Family obligations can prevent men and women from developing new friendships, advancing in their work and having time for themselves, or they can propel them into new activities, new insights and shared intimacies. Some of the fathers we interviewed treated their child care as yet another job to be fitted into their busy schedule and conscientiously set aside time to be with their children. Others seemed to be able to integrate the family activities into their lives in ways that appeared to enhance many other activities. Although, they too, might set aside special times to be with their children, they were more likely to include the children in their own daily activities or to use the time with the children for activities which they enjoyed and might not otherwise be able to find time for. For these men, the children were not yet another obligation, but a special pleasure:

"I can only be myself with my children," one father said. "A kid is a ticket to being a kid again," said another.

To better understand how child-care obligations affect the lifestyles of men who live outside of marriage, we asked the men in our sample about their housing arrangements, finances and work lives. We also asked them about their plans for remarriage and the possibility of additional children. We were interested in attitudes towards the conventional nuclear family of men who have had the experience of child rearing under the stressful conditions of marital breakup.

Housing

At the time of separation it is usually the man who leaves the family residence. The move is made at the height of the emotional crisis. The subsequent choice of housing is an important decision for a separated father. In the beginning, there is a tendency towards makeshift and temporary arrangements: moving in with friends, putting a couch in the office or renting a room in some not very desirable location can be viewed as an expression of resistance to the new situation. It serves to emphasize the sense of inner discomfort and disruption.

Setting up a household requires time and energy as well as money, and many men feel too insecure both emotionally and financially in those early days of separation to make this effort. It is very likely that during the first year of a separation a man will move several times. Some of these moves represent a range of fantasies, from a rapid recreation of "family" life with roommates, friends or extended family, to living out the glamorous image of a swinging bachelor in his "pad."

The resultant lack of residential stability makes child-care scheduling difficult. Many men are reluctant to bring their children to these first, inadequate, residences. In the end it is often the desire to establish a routine of child care that becomes an important determinant of the choice of lifestyle and type of housing.

Although most of the fathers we interviewed had been separated for a minimum of two years, close to half had been at their present address for less than a year. Another 40 percent had been living in the same place for two years. The more child care responsibility the fathers have the more likely they are to report residential stability. For full-custody fathers the mean time at their present residence was thirty-two months, while for the other three groups of fathers it was twenty-three months, seventeen, and sixteen months respectively.

Most of the men in our sample lived in rented apartements (61 percent). A little over one-third (38 percent) lived in a one- or two-family house, which they usually owned. This latter group consisted mostly of full-custody fathers, half of whom owned the houses they occupied, and half-time fathers, a fourth of whom owned their residences.

The decision about whether to live alone or with other adults is often based on financial as well as emotional considerations. One of the respondents who took care of his child half-time and owned his own house was forced to rent out rooms in order to meet the mortgage payments without increasing his work hours. He was not happy with the arrangement and wished that he could afford to have the house all to himself. Other men, however, had deliberately chosen to live with other adults, often men in the same life situation, so as to have support and company for themselves and their children. Nearly half the respondents reported living alone (46 percent).

The group of fathers who saw their children least frequently were most likely to be in the "alone" group (61 percent). Another 38 percent of the total sample reported living with a roommate or in some other form of cooperative arrangement. Most of the men in this last group had shared custody (half-time).

How the children's time with the father is spent is determined to a large degree by living arrangements. The less time the child spends with the father, the more likely it is that no other adults or playmates are included. Even the proportion of time spent playing alone or watching TV while in the father's care decreases as the time with the father decreases. While both the full-time and joint-custody fathers are apt to consider time spent in household chores and other caretaking activities as time devoted to their children, the visiting fathers spend more time in special activities alone with their offspring. The concentrated attention of the visiting father who is making up for lost time represents a somewhat distorted picture of a parent-child relationship. Many men are reluctant to "spoil" that time with disagreements or discipline. After acceding to all the demands of the children, many fathers breathe a guilty sigh of relief when the visit is over.

Lifestyle Limitations

All fathers experience child care as limiting. Time alone and time with other adults, especially dating, are the major areas of limitations. Other expressed limitations, in decreasing order, are: trips, work, vacations, educational opportunities and remarriage. It is interesting to note that while dating is viewed as very limited because of child-care obligations, few men felt that child care limited their chances for remarriage. Full-time fathers and joint-custody fathers differ little from each other in their sense of limitation, but they report being more limited than is the case for part-time fathers. The situation is reversed for "vacations," where full-time fathers can avail themselves of the help of ex-wives or other adults in order to vacation alone, while part-time fathers often spend all vacation time with their children.

In several instances joint-custody fathers view themselves as more limited than full-time fathers, especially when it comes to dating and time alone. This may be due to the fact that men who do not have full-time child care are less likely to have regular assistants such as housekeepers or babysitters. It is also possible that by leading a half-and-half lifestyle—having one foot, so to speak, in the world of "singleness" and the other in the world of family—they may find a need for frequent readjustment and never quite accept the periodical restrictions on their freedom.

The more child-care obligations the father has, the less likely he is to date a woman with children of her own. Perhaps having responsibility for two sets of children is more than a relationship can withstand. In fact, when asked if their relationship with new partners conflicts with their child-care obligations, half or more of each group reported such conflicts.

The conflict was least frequent for joint-custody fathers (39 percent). These men are likely to live with other adults and date women who are single and childless. It may be that these fathers limit dating to their child-free time.

When we asked the fathers about the specific activities they had been forced to give up as a result of child-care obligations, social life was mentioned first, sports second. "I miss a real tough game of tennis," said one father. "Now it seems I'm always playing with children." It may be that these are the activities most easy to forego when other obligations intervene. It is difficult to tell whether the perceived reduction in social activities has any objective validity or is measured against a fantasy of a "social whirl" which might be possible if the children were not there. The individuals in our sample show a great range of sociability: from a full-custody father who divides his time between work and child care and has time for few other activities, to a part-time father who lives with his lover, dates two other women and still feels he "would date a lot more" if his children were not with him.

Work Styles

The integration of work and child care has long been the bane of the working mother. It also becomes a problem for fathers who take care of children. One full-time father in our sample was unemployed, having opted for Aid to Dependent Families. Another ten of the full-time fathers and six of the half-time fathers worked a somewhat reduced workweek. Eighty-three percent of all the men interviewed worked full-time or more.

Flexibility in work hours was more likely to be reported by half-time fathers. Income also fluctuated with child-care time. Full- and half-time fathers averaged considerably less income than less involved men (see Table 8).

The conflicts between work and child care experienced by these fathers are similar to those reported frequently by single mothers. Men who during their married lives expected their families to adjust to the demands of their work suddenly find themselves having to coordinate and juggle the schedules of work and child care. Here accepted standards of nine-to-five duties begin to seem unreasonable. As one father employed by a large engineering firm told us:

My boss is old fashioned: he does not care what work I actually do, but he must see me there from nine to five. It is very inconvenient for me, and I knew I could get as much or more work done on a more flexible schedule, but he would not hear of it.

Other fathers who had more work independence found that it was their own expectations they had to overcome.

I had to give up this image of being a scholar, sitting in the library till all hours of the night. Others in my department did that and they were family men too. But pretty soon I only came in to teach and did some extra work when [his son] was not with me. I started to enjoy being at home. After all, he would grow up and I might have missed all that; the library would always be there.

The fathers report passing up promotions that might mean a move away from the children, reducing their work hours and choosing work for its compatibility with the demands of child care. We must not underestimate the importance of this change for highly achieving professional men. Socialization for career performance is one of the outstanding features of male identity (Pleck, 1974). Much has been written about the general importance of work as a source of well-being for men—work as a source of life purpose (Morse and Weiss, 1955), as a prized self-image (Wilensky, 1966), and as a validating experience (Rainwater, 1974).

The reduction of involvement in work has two sources. On the one hand, it is a practical response to the overload of demands on the father's time. Even with day-care services, babysitters, and the help of the extended family (although the last is rare for middle-class men), much time and energy is absorbed by the child's needs. On the other hand, as indicated later, eventually child care becomes defined as another job for which the father has contracted. When this happens the rewards of doing that job well and feeling competent in it begin to compete with work satisfaction, thus reducing the salience of occupational role for the men.

General analyses of work and family in modern America can be summarized as accepting the centrality of work for determining the quality of family life. Dissatisfaction with work is thought to lead to an unsatisfactory family life. This analysis tends to be reversed for women—that is, for women, personal satisfactions are seen as dependent on their marital and fertility status, motherhood being the source of major identity. Consequently, the influence of family demands on career decisions has been extensively studied for women but not for men.

To view it in a somewhat different way: women may resist the demands of occupational socialization by the legitimacy of their participation in the family. Men, on the other hand, find little support in rejecting the demands of the work world on behalf of family functions. A woman worker may more easily state that she will not accept overtime because "her children need her" or "her husband does not like it." The same reasons stated by a male worker undermine the expected masculine image of autonomy and independence. Thus, both the desire and the attempt to restructure family participation on the part of a married man may be severely restricted by his own work expectations, the expectations of family members, and inflexible work obligations. Pleck (1974) views the current structure of the male occupational role as a major limitation of the sex-role change in the family.

The divorced father finds himself in a somewhat different situation. His child-care involvement is motivated by the fear of losing a relationship with his children. His newly acquired parenting role—whether as a weekend, half-time, or single father—is a new legal or contractual obligation. Parenting which in a marriage was likely to come second to work obligations is now a legitimate function *on a par* with the demands of work. In fact, it acquires many of the characteristics of work, and fathers begin to develop competence, recognize cues for judging themselves as competent, and experience the familiar rewards of a job well done.

Learning to overcome the initial feelings of inadequacy which many fathers experience when doing "women's work" can be more easily done when the child-care tasks are seen as a legitimate new assignment to be "worked on." New definitions of fathering have to be developed. "Getting a divorce really made me pause and think what is my role as a father; am I any good at raising the children? I often found myself lacking." But only at first. With additional experience comes competence and self-assurance.

For men, the issue of parenting by themselves is the issue of competence and the ways in which they understand competent performance in caring for and relating to children. Women evaluate parenting more often through their emotional relationship with the child.

The issue of competence and efficacy dominates the self-image of males. The cultural image of competence is cold and impersonal, but it also can be a way to think about feelings and to begin to learn how to function interpersonally. A man who begins to parent and who can meet the purely practical needs of children—bathing, feeding, getting them to school on time—begins to feel more effective. This sense of effectiveness translates both into his good feelings about the children and into the good feelings which he learns that the children have about him. The crisis often comes when the needs to be satisfied are purely emotional—the temper tantrum is the most trying event for a newly independent father.

It's when she cried and I didn't know what to do for her; I didn't understand it. So I would try to figure it out by trial and error. Did I do something bad? I go through a series of hypotheses. It took a while but I finally learned how to figure out what's bothering her. I feel a lot better now. I can get an idea of what's upsetting her now. I also can get her to tell me what's wrong and I can generally do something about it.

In describing the same problem, another father contrasted it with the way he has seen his wife handle it.

My wife is different. What she does is to just somehow intuit what's upsetting our son. Or sometimes she just will say, "you feel sad," and not need to know the reason but just deal with the sadness. I don't know if I can do that. I have to understand what is wrong.

Once the feelings of competence begin to be introduced into the area of dealing with children's emotions, reinforced by the child's well-being, the whole area of emotions becomes less threatening for men. Each father can develop his own criteria for doing a good job as a father in the way he relates to the children.

For men socialized to believe that feelings must be kept hidden and are a barrier to effective functioning, experiencing competency in this area can be a source of positive self-regard.

Suddenly I found I could really do it. I saw that I could take care of the girls and respond to their emotional needs as well as run the house.

Bringing the criteria of work performance, familiar to men, to the parenting role appears to make men at ease with their new obligations. It also gives the parenting role an external legitimacy and internal satisfaction which undermines the impact of work socialization for men, and frees them to develop a more individually determined balance of work and family commitment.

What remains to be seen is whether these individual adjustments can be maintained over time against the pressures of employers' expectations, especially when new relationships with women may reduce the father's family obligations.

Our original interest in separated fathers was based on the hypothesis that the structural demands of child care would force changes in the lives of men, with the result that their behavioral and personality profiles might look more like those of women.

We had not anticipated the extension of that change to a new family configuration. It may be that the emphasis on boundaries and control, which is the result of male socialization in relation to work, when carried to the area of the family has positive consequences. The same patterns, assimilated by women, may provide them with a basis for freeing themselves from some of the negative aspects of the mothering function and female socialization for family membership.

Remarriage and Fertility

The questions of future remarriage and fertility plans for men have not been addressed either in studies of families or studies of male lifestyles or identity. Our data suggests that these are present and important concerns in the lives of separated fathers who have already had the experience of marrying and having a family. Faced with the disruption of that commonly expected lifestyle, they are now in a position to make new decisions with experience and forethought.

We find that 63.7 percent, almost two-thirds of the sample, when asked if they want to remarry, respond affirmatively. Quarter-time fathers are least likely to express a desire for remarriage. This is the same group of men who are least likely to be involved in a new relationship with a woman, and also the least likely to rely on a new woman lover for assistance with their children. The quarter-time fathers who do express a desire to remarry, when asked about the possibility of having more children, leave this decision up to their future spouse. These men consider themselves to be in an uncomfortable and unsatisfactory lifestyle, and seem to have the greatest difficulty taking control of their lives. It is very likely that this inability to come to terms with their new situation, and to feel in control of their lives, makes them reluctant or unable to engage in new relationships or even to speculate about such a possibility.

Over 58 percent of the total sample answered "yes" to having more children in the future. Comparing the groups who responded both "yes" to remarriage, and "yes" to future children, we find that marriage and fertility are separate issues for men in our study. This seems different from the way these matters are usually addressed by individuals contemplating their first marriage—that is, the men who already had experience with children view their participation in a decision to have more children in a more immediate way than is true of men who have not had the experience. Within our sample, more involved fathers (joint- and full-care) were more likely to give personal (i.e., "I love children") reasons for wanting more children, as opposed to the less involved fathers who saw the decision to have additional children as dependent on the attitudes and desires of their future spouses.

This is not to say that women are not important in making this decision for all groups. Men who are involved with single and childless women are more likely to report desiring more children in the future. This suggests that there is an interaction between level of care, the father's individual liking for children, and the possibility of current sexual partners wanting children. For full- and joint-custody men the remarriage plans are most influenced by the father's concern for the compatibility between his existing children and the contemplated partner. Less involved fathers stress, instead, the importance of compatibility between the future marriage partners and themselves.

We also found, to our surprise, that many men answered "yes" to our question about their desire to have more children and "no" to the question about remarriage. Fathers who were highly involved with their children were more likely to want to have more children. Yet the level of involvement with children shows no correlation with plans to remarry. This highly involved group is also less likely to report conflict with the ex-wife. Conversely the men who do report a high degree of conflict with their ex-spouses are less likely to want to have more children in the future. Since the conflict is likely to be over issues of child care, these men see child rearing as detrimental to a good relationship between marriage partners. Inasmuch as they find it possible to cooperate with their ex-spouses around child care, they might feel less need to find new marriage partners who would share the parenting. In fact, as we will see later, there might be concern that a new marriage will upset the postdivorce arrangement.

In analyzing the variations in attitudes towards remarriage and re-familying, we find that the responses can be grouped in the following categories:

a. Men who view the children as primarily the responsibility of a woman and inevitably desired by her. Their view of marriage is that you cannot expect to have an enduring heterosexual relationship without "giving her" children.

b. Men who view the begetting of children as a natural part of the relationship between a man and a woman and of equal importance to them both. These men want to have children not just because they believe it is the woman's expectations, but because they themselves enjoy children, want to be with children and feel that important personal growth occurs for them in the relationship with their children.

c. And finally we find a group of men who believe that their marriages run aground and continue to suffer from conflict over child care. (Most of the conflict between the ex-spouses is in fact over child-care arrangements and financial support.) These men are anxious to remarry, but the lesson they feel they have learned is that the coming of children alters the relationship. They are looking for partners who are compatible with them, and when they find one, they would rather not, as one father expressed it, "mess up a good relationship by having children."

There is a relationship between attitudes towards one's ex-spouse and the desire to remarry. On the whole, the men in our sample do not score highly in our measures of negative attitudes towards the ex-wives. Only 32 percent of the sample scored above the median. However, those men who offer fewer negative descriptions of the ex-wives are less likely to want to remarry. On the other hand, those who do view their ex-wives in very negative terms are more likely to want to remarry, but less likely to want to have more children. The same is true for men who express a great deal of conflict with their ex-wives.

This gives us a group of responses from men who hold a very positive view of, and perhaps, by implication, a continuing attachment to, their ex-wives. These men say that they do not wish to remarry, but if that ever happened, they would like to have more children. It seems, therefore, that marriage is viewed strongly enough as a positive arrangement for one's lifestyle so that men who have not had good luck with their partners the first time are quite willing to try again with a new partner.

Given a bad marital experience, however, fathers are much less likely to want to have more children. Whether the floundering of marriage can be ascribed to the presence of children or not has been debated in many studies. It is difficult to have a clear understanding of this, since by the time a marriage is likely to grow problematic (five to seven years) there are likely to be children present. Difficulties between the partners themselves can easily be ascribed to the parenting relationship. Immature, or insecure, adults who would find it difficult to function in a sustained adult relationship, find it difficult, it seems, to care for children and each other at the same time.

Our data indicate that a negative marital experience affects attitudes towards fertility more than it does attitudes towards remarriage. Men who experienced less conflict and who are involved with children plan to choose mates who are compatible with that involvement, and with their desire to have more children.

The issue of conflict with the ex-wife is partly obscured by the confounding with the general functioning of men. From our case studies we have some indications that certain men avoid conflict by being distant, detached, and generally loners. Their low level of involvement and expressiveness makes them less likely candidates for commitment or involvement either as fathers or husbands. Some of the visiting fathers fall into that category, and although they would like to remarry it is more difficult for them to form relationships. They show little change or growth in dealing with the issues of separation, and merely wish to reestablish a conventional family.

The full-time fathers, on the other hand, view remarriage in more practical terms: as a way to be able to share some of their burden of child care, and to overcome the limitations to their social life with other adults. Their view on future fatherhood appears also more practical and has to do with the number of children they already have, their finances and other realities of child care. On the whole, however, their attitude is one of sympathy to children and to the state of fatherhood.

The Changing Patterns of Intimacy

The postdivorce lifestyle involved an extensive resocialization about relationships both with children and with other adults. Many men consciously experiment with new patterns of intimacy, especially if they feel their marriage was repressive or cold. Some men, in making themselves known to their children as "real people," wish to include the sense of themselves as warm and sexual. Others worry that a love relationship apart from the children might add to the children's sense of betrayal and isolation from the father. Still others, however, are uneasy about the possible sense of competition between the new lover and the children which might force the father into a serious conflict of loyalties. Thus the issue of having a lover sleep over at the father's house when the children are there is often quite pivotal. It makes the father accountable for the relationship to the children as well as to the ex-wife, and it also makes public a certain degree of commitment to the partner which a newly divorced man may feel reluctant to make. Many men feel strongly that such a situation must not be allowed. Of course the more time a father spends with his children the more likely he is to include his lover. Three-fourths of the men we interviewed did allow their lovers to stay overnight. The same men were more likely to allow their woman friends greater participation in child care.

At the time of separation it is difficult for many men to imagine that they could ever again feel closeness with a woman and plan a future together. Even men who are involved with another sexual partner at the time of separation are wary of commitment. In the case of men who did not desire or initiate the divorce proceedings, the process of psychological separation is even slower. These men often have hopes and expectations of reconciliation which to an objective observer appear clearly unrealistic. While the legal separation or divorce decree entitles a man to take up his single life, many are unaware that the psychological divorce may take much longer. Bohannan (1970), in describing the "six stations" of divorce, places psychic divorce as the very last, defining it as a slow process of regaining individual autonomy. Waller (1967) also describes final estrangement between the ex-spouses as complete only some time after the partners have entered new social worlds.

The divorced men themselves describe this time as one of depression or apathy. They may be tired or rushed, transient in their living arrangements, or burdened with child care. All these become reasons to defend against an immediate involvement with a new partner. Somehow, however, new relationships do get established. We know that approximately 50 percent of the people who get divorced remarry within three years (Glick and Norton, 1977), so that not long after the separation—needing to reassert themselves as attractive males—men begin "dating." The term "dating" is used self-consciously and evokes all the insecurities, hesitations, and posturing that are part of its adolescent origins. It is a time of "trying out" a new self, even though most divorced people do not really enter the world of single people, but that of the formerly married (Hunt, 1966; Cox, 1978).

The relationships retain the status of dating for as long as the dating couple avoids the formulation of any mutual ties or obligations, even though at any given moment in time the date might fulfill all the functions of a temporary marriage mate. It is important to the partners that they maintain separate residences and have separate friends and activities. The purpose of the separateness is to underline the "casual" nature of the relationship. The man is reestablishing his *independence,* which might be easily threatened. It is understood that the relationship could be easily terminated if either party so desires. There should be no mutual property, no need to explain to the children why "he" or "she" is not there on Sundays anymore—in other words, as little as possible which might be reminiscent of the marital breakup.

It is difficult if not impossible to adhere to such a definition of dating for a long time with one person. Deliberately or not, communalities develop; friends and children begin to expect the presence of the date; comfortable habits set in. Men who explicitly and determinably wish to prevent such a development find themselves in the peculiar, and often hard to explain, situation of wanting to break off a relationship precisely because it feels comfortable, and because they are beginning to depend on it for both emotional sustenance and real help around the house. The experience leaves the woman bewildered and bitter. "What went wrong?" She wonders why he wants to break off just when everything is going so well, when the children have finally gotten to like her, and they've been so comfortable together. It is not often that she can get a satisfactory explanation. "I am just not ready," the man is likely to say obliquely, or else he disagrees over some small matter to create opportunity to divest himself of the encroaching commitment.

To understand this dynamic, which pervades the patterns of dating and the course of developing and changing relationships, we must remember that issues of power or control, and of dependency, are the major issues roused by the proceedings of marital breakup. Fathers who spend time with their young children after divorce have an opportunity to work out these issues in their parenting relationship, making the parental relationship an important source of personal reconstruction (Keshet and Rosenthal, 1978).

Several authors have discussed the relationship between power and dependency (Blau, 1955, 1964; Thibaut and Kelley, 1959; Emerson, 1962). Emerson (1962) proposes a simple formula in which the power of A over B equals the dependency of B on A. Kemper (1972) views these as central variables in any analysis of adult relationships. As we have stated elsewhere (Keshet and Rosenthal, 1978: 1), fathers after divorce often give a great deal of power to their children and become dependent on them emotionally. Following the natural status position of father and child, this situation can be gradually adjusted in accord with the strengthening self-image of the father. The situation is different vis-à-vis an emotional involvement with a new lover. The father's newly emerged independence is threatened because he recognizes aspects of real dependency in his parental responsibilities. Furthermore, to accept and recognize this dependency may undermine his still-vulnerable masculinity. Thus, the father who is in fact engaged in the process of personal growth through his child-care adjustments is wary of being interfered with through a new relationship with a woman.

A woman who is socialized to be responsive and helpful as an important part of her intimate relationship is most vulnerable to rejection in this situation. She is often surprised to find that the man she was interested in becomes involved in a relationship with another woman who appears to "care" for him much less—that is, offers less housekeeping help. Given this configuration, divorce may, in part, serve the need for autonomy in the area of emotional and parental coping allowing necessary competence to emerge. Once a man feels good about himself, and secure in his familial capabilities, he may be much more available for a new love relationship.

Dating

Relationships of short duration, or multiple dating, serve to enforce the barriers between new potential partners. All the men interviewed had, shortly after separation, dated more than one woman at a time. The pattern, which appears to repeat, begins with a fairly intense involvement immediately after separation which has the quality of a "port in a storm." The woman in question is often more a confidante than a lover: she listens to complaints against the ex-spouse, the legal system, and whatever other forces seem to conspire against the newly divorced man. She is a witness to his insecurities and a focus in groupings for a new identity. When that first stage has passed, however, and some sort of emotional equilibrium is reached, this is rarely the relationship that lasts. For men anxious to try out new powers, the woman who has witnessed his setbacks is not the ideal partner. The time of quiet recuperation with one sympathetic and supportive woman is often followed by frequent and varied dating. After the first year, relationships become more exclusive and of longer duration and may lead to a more serious partnership or cohabitation.

This pattern seems as true for men who have a committed lover waiting for them at the time of the marital breakup as for those whose failed marriage leave them with no one to turn to. It is only after a period of experimentation and heightened dating activity that some men return to their original extramarital lover who may have been the impetus for the divorce. We conclude from our case studies that the patterns of dating following marital separation are not accidental. They appear to be a replay of the unresolved issues of adolescence, such as separation, individualization, differentiation, and finally commitment.

Commitment often becomes defined by sexual exclusivity. The refusal of such exclusivity is another means of delaying such commitment, even when the couple is explicitly or effectively living together. Some couples have an explicit understanding that other sexual partners are permissible for both. Others have not made such an explicit agreement, but neither have they ruled it out. This ambiguity about the permissibility of other sexual encounters reflects, on one hand, the changing attitudes towards fidelity within marriage (Roy and Roy, 1970; O'Neill and O'Neill, 1972), and, on the other, the uses of promiscuity as power; it has been shown that the mate who is less concerned with monogamy and pursues other sexual relationships has power over the partner who desires sexual fidelity and is not promiscuous.

It is also likely that men use their prerogative of seeking out new partners less out of real sexual interest than as a reminder both to themselves and their primary partner that they are not in fact married. Such a reminder provides the safety margin that an earlier stage required the actual breaking off of the dating relationship.

Characteristics of New Partners

It was common for the men we interviewed to date women with certain social characteristics. They were frequently considerably younger than the men, of similar social class, and, whether single, divorced, or separated, were unlikely to have children of their own. Only a third of the respondents reported forming "serious relationships" with women who had children. Although such relationships were more common for men in the early stages of separation and seem to represent a desire to reconstruct the marriage configuration, they generally did not last. Whatever the attraction of the ready-made family—the woman whose life is set up for child care, who can usually include the children of the separated father in the weekly activities, and who has a child-equipped house—it does not last. In the long run, there are too many difficulties in coordination and planning for the two partners. A relationship based on the man's needs as a part-time father rarely coincides with what he wants as a man recovering a sense of his own desirability.

I dated a woman with children and it was fairly complicated. She had a time commitment to her own children. Her kids entered into our relationship; so did mine. We each had to relate to and like each other's kids as well as liking and relating to each other.

One father dated a woman because she had a station wagon and on weekends they could all pile into the car and go on picnics which she prepared. Another man dated a woman whose functioning as a mother he admired and realized that he used the time to learn from her how to behave with his own children. In the end, however, the father's own sense of himself as a man apart from his child-care responsibilities tends to assert itself.

Dating women of similar social class characteristics, often of similar work interests or professional concerns, increases the opportunity to separate a sense of oneself as a single adult from that of oneself as a part-time parent. This is true both emotionally and in terms of time flexibility. Many of the fathers needed the support of this love relationship immediately after delivering the children to the ex-spouse—a time of more-than-ordinary stress.

Dating women who did not have children of their own allowed for more time flexibility. Since most fathers take their children on the weekend, dating a woman without children of her own made it easier to plan the time alone on the weekdays when neither had other obligations. It also made it possible for the woman to be of company and assistance to the father when the children were with him and to sleep over on the nights when the children were not there. Divorced women with similar child-care arrangements were likely to resent having to spend time with someone else's children on the weekends when they themselves were free from child care. One father complained that he had stopped dating a woman with children partly because it was so difficult to have time alone together.

Refamilying

Eighty percent of all divorced people eventually remarry. Remarriage often follows a period of cohabitation. By the end of the second year of separation many men are seriously considering living with a woman. Although the stereotype is that it is the woman who pressures for commitment and stability during a dating relationship, we cannot state conclusively from our data that this is so. First of all, we find that the arrangements for time together are often difficult when the man has children who spend some of their time with him. It has been the general pattern in our newly sexually free groups that single people may cohabit with each other on a part-time basis. Gone are the days when there was nowhere to go to spend the night for many sophisticated urban singles. The back of the car, the nervous motel registrations, the phony wedding ring are for the most part just a spectre of the 1950s. "Your place or mine?" is the current style.

In the general course of events it is usually the man who is likely to stay over at his date's place. There are many reasons for this: women are more likely to care about their environments and have a home which feels and is more comfortable. There will be clean sheets and something for breakfast; this is more than one can expect to find in many a bachelor pad. Many women do not want the experience of having to wash a week of dishes or help put away accumulated papers before they can relax in a romantic atmosphere. Others feel safer and more relaxed in their own house. So her house it is. Pretty soon the man, if he becomes a steady date, finds himself spending more and more time at the house of his lover. He leaves some clothes behind, then some work, and before long he has more or less explicitly moved in. When the decision to live together is made, that is where they stay. Sometimes a stray roommate will move out to allow for additional space, and sometimes the new couple will hunt for a place of their own.

This is much less likely to be the case with the separated fathers. The father feels under some pressure to create a home, at least part-time, for his children. He is therefore more careful about his surroundings, and more settled. This is especially true at least in the second year of the separation, when the child-care schedule has become regular and stable. He must spend time at his house, at least when the children are there. He is likely to want to be there at other times as well, first of all because they might want to reach him, but most importantly because he has put an effort into creating a home. His sense of home is already divided between the house that he and his ex-wife had shared and his new domicile, and he may not wish to fraction it further.

The newly separated man, anxious to make his quarters feel like home for himself and his children, is less likely to make himself a part-time inhabitant of his lover's house. It is she, therefore, who must come to his house—a situation that she may be unused to but one that many women do in fact find intriguing or different. She is likely to find there a much more domesticated man, one who is aware of whether or not the dishes are washed, one who does not automatically assume that she will take on the homemaking (in its true sense) responsibilities, one who may in fact be somewhat possessive of his newly acquired housekeeping skills. Many fathers are still proving to their ex-spouses and children that they are competent parents, and still proving to themselves that they can maintain control over their domestic and parental lives. Their unwillingness to return to the division of roles which characterized their marriage may present a very different possibility of coexistence to a new female lover.

A great deal has been written recently on gender roles within a family. Dual-career families have been of special interest because the possible conflicts engendered by the interference with the traditional division of labor between husband and wife "provides us with a glimpse of emerging family dynamics" (Gordon, 1978). The studies all emphasize the continuing responsibility of the woman for the smooth running of the household and the care of the children, even when the wife's career commitments make sharing of the family tasks either a reasonable expectation or an explicit decision (Holmstrom, 1972; Rapoport and Rapoport, 1971). Child-care responsibilities are specifically assigned to the wife. In a study of 33 families, Polema and Garland (1971) found only one family which they were willing to describe as egalitarian in that respect. The willing assumption of the child care, as well as conflict and guilt engendered over any interference with mothering, has been ascribed to the socialization of women, which emphasizes their family roles (Reiss, 1965; Rubin, 1976).

The case of men and their children cohabiting with a new sexual partner provides us with an opportunity to view a family situation which is almost the reverse of the traditional marriage. The children are first and foremost the responsibility of the father. The female partner is usually economically independent, having work of her own which existed prior to the family situation and which continues to have priority. Not only are the house and children a major responsibility of the father, but he also views it as his function to coordinate the members of the household and make sure that they feel good about each other. This is the "expressive" leadership function described by Parsons and Bales (1955) as the very core of the wife's role in the family. He retains his dominant status, however, both in the family as head of the household and in the larger society. The woman's socialization may lead her to expect to take on the mother and wife roles, but the structural conditions of the particular circumstance force her to deal with these expectations in a new and innovative way. We have here, then, within the family, a microcosm of an experimental situation where the roles are reversed, without a corresponding major change in the wider social structure.

For the woman in that situation, the wife and mother roles are an extension of her love relationship with the man and are mediated by it. When the direct love relationship with the father is terminated, so is her role vis-à-vis the house and children. This is not unlike the traditional priority of the husband role for men, and the mediation of their fathering through the relationship with the wife (Pleck, 1974).

Younger, childless women, who are more likely to have grown up with expectations of independence and self-assertion, are better equipped emotionally to function within this configuration. It is not unlikely that divorced men who have this mode of coping with their new state gravitate toward this type of woman. Men who, on the other hand, are anxious to replicate their previous marital arrangements may be more likely to marry more traditional women or ones who have children of their own from a previous marriage.

Adjustments to Cohabitation

The transition from a dating relationship—where the woman has her own home to retreat to and functions more like a guest in the father's house—to cohabitation is a very major transition because it puts a strain on the equilibrium that has been worked out. Women who have learned to be sensitive to the autonomy needs of the man in and out of the house, and to their own secondary position within the new family, may find that their natural inclination or expectation to take over the family respon-

sibilities becomes very strong where the cues for separateness
are diminished. In other words, once moved in, can the not-quite
stepmother maintain her nontraditional role within the household configuration? And can the man in turn respect her autonomy and maintain his own functioning as the responsible
parent despite the clear temptation to increase the reliance on
the new partner to a degree which might naturally slip into a
relationship reminiscent of the discarded marriage? The couple
must evidence a great deal of self-awareness and commitment to
the new lifestyle in order to defend themselves against these
changes.

The line between commitment to the children expected from a
new partner and the participation in child-care responsibility
must be most carefully balanced. This is probably one of the
most dramatic aspects of the new relationship, and the most
frequent source of tension.

There are many aspects of role reversal entailed in sharing
parenting with a divorced father. The tone of the relationship is
generally set by the fact that the new woman moves into a house
already occupied by the father. The house was chosen for its
suitability for his child-care obligations, proximity to the children's mother or school, and a space for their visits, and has
been tested by his developing and routinizing his parenting tasks
there. If a move is made it is usually for the same reasons as the
above—that is, the father's parenting obligations set the
perimeters of their decisions.

Since the man's free time is often planned with child care in
mind, the extra energy and attention required by the new
arrangement often come in conflict with the established routine.
Vacations, weekends, and other times which normally an adult
couple would have free for themselves are often the very times
when children are most present. The sense that the man is not
fully available, practically and emotionally, and that his child-
care obligations take priority over his relationship to his lover
are the most commonly reported sources of conflict in the first
months of cohabitation. Often the separation of time alone and
time with the children becomes more difficult than when the
couple lived apart. If conflict between the father and the children

develops, it is more difficult for the new woman to simply absent herself and provide the space for the father to solve it.

Fathers are especially conscious of needing to reassure the children, and perhaps their ex-spouses as well, that the new partner will not usurp the father's time and attention or even the physical space in the house. Many men admitted favoring the children when their lover first moved in. It was difficult to distinguish how much such behavior is meant to reassure the children and how much it is due to their own insecurity in the new situation. The children provide an excuse for creating some real and emotional barriers against the increasing intimacy.

Men who have only recently gained control over their children and a sense of competence in their parenting roles are generally happy to share housekeeping tasks, but are much less eager to relinquish their direct relationship with the children. "I would consult with [her] about helping me with child care, but basically I was still the parent and they were still my responsibility." There was, in fact, often a special effort on the part of the father to let the children know that he, the father, would continue to be the "real" parent and was not abdicating his rights and responsibilities vis-à-vis the children. At the same time the cohabiting partner had lost the status of a guest in the house which might have given her special privileges and instead had assumed the more modest role of a helper. This is the new family socialization which takes place and further reinforces the role reversal we have described. The new woman is *not*, strictly speaking, a mother substitute, because in most cases the children have a perfectly adequate mother. Instead, she shares the fathering role, emulates his behavior, relies on his approval. As the husband once babysat for his wife, she now "babysits" for him. The traditional fatherly functions of driving children to school or picking them up are often taken over by the new partner.

Most fathers see such activities as *help for them*, not as direct caretaking of the child.

It was really nice to have help when I needed it. But I never lost sight of the fact that the children were my responsibility and my enjoyment too.

Sometimes it was really nice not to have anyone else around but me and my children.

Such confessions are painful to hear for the new family member. Fathers are both deliberate and explicit in directing and limiting the amount of interaction between their new partners and the children. Only when a struggle ensued did these situations become more clarified. The demands of the new partner had to be made on emotional grounds, and their bargaining power was perhaps the lowest as compared to the needs of both the children and the father.

Kitty [partner] often resented doing things related to the children. I did not realize what it was I was expecting or how much help I was actually getting until I asked her to pick up the children and she refused.

Faith accused me of shutting her out when the kids were here. She said I was always limiting what she could do with them. I thought it had to do with not wanting to impose on her, but now I think it had more to do with authority and control. Funny how these old things keep popping up.

In general, the defense presented by the fathers as to why they seemed intent on preserving a distance between their partners and their children had to do with the desire to protect the children from the upheavals of another separation should their new relationship prove to be temporary. In fact, however, it is likely that the fathers were protecting themselves. Having evolved a relationship with the children where their presence and caring was central and expected, as opposed to the often peripheral relationship which fathers have in intact marriages, these men were unwilling to chance a reversal. The presence of a woman in the household evoked the memory of a household where the woman was emotionally central in the parenting relationship, and this threatened the man with a possibility of such a reversal. Many of the men were unsure whether in case of real competition for their children's affection, their partner might not win because of their sex. On the other hand, the temptation to hand over the burdens and trials of child-care responsibility likewise threatened the newly developed parental identity. This resulted in the somewhat exaggerated effort to assert their authority as a biological parent.

And, finally, we found an unwillingness to share the already seemingly divided affection and loyalty of the children with yet another adult. Many men only too willing to share the drudgery of daily household tasks would have thought twice about sharing the rewards of their parenting.

It was difficult for many of the fathers clearly to define a role for their partner that did not in some way seem to displace either themselves or their ex-spouses. In many cases there was a great fear of engendering even the slightest conflict between the partner and the ex-spouse, and possibly threatening the often informal child-care agreement.

In the majority of cases, the respondents definitely defined their partner as a helper, but not as a parent or even a parent substitute, thus explicitly limiting their emotional involvement with the child and reemphasizing their own importance as a biological parent.

I am not looking for a mother substitute for [daughter]. She already has a mother that she is very close to.

We are struggling about the extent to which she [partner] wants to be involved [with the children] and can be psychologically involved given her position [here the father emphasized the insecurity and possible transience of the new relationship].

The children themselves participated in many of these struggles. They, too, were wary of forming new dependencies on people whose permanence and status in their lives was not to be trusted. They were often reluctant to allow the partner to care for them, even after having known them for years. They competed for the father's attention and protected their special relationship. They often rejected the attempts of the new parent surrogate to establish emotional closeness, affection, or direction. All respondents reported such experiences of rejection of their partners. Fathers of male children reported this more frequently than fathers of female children.

Despite the resistance, despite the caution and the jealousies, somehow during the first year of living together emotional closeness does become possible between the new woman and the children. Affection becomes openly shared; children freely express their concern for and interest in the newly accepted family member. The relationship appears more mutual and independent of the father's mediation. The women are able to relate directly to the children and view them as their friends. In many cases, the fathers, having overcome their initial possessiveness, are able to encourage the developing bonds with the children and can now appreciate, unthreatened, the contribution that their partners make to the care of the children.

Jean [daughter] said that she loved Wendy [partner]. But she didn't know what to do about it because Wendy was not her mother. She and Wendy were able to talk about it and they both seemed happy. And I was glad that Jean felt that way and glad that they could talk about it.

The kids like her to kiss them before going to sleep, but they want me to get them ready for bed and put them to sleep. Still they accept her and love her.

The acknowledgment of an independent relationship between the lover and the children indicates a definite shift in the woman's role in the household and indicates the growth of new family-like relationships.

At this point the partner becomes much more active in the parenting. Fathers become freer in discussing problems of child rearing with their partners and consulting them on issues of discipline and authority. Discussion of styles of parenting and standards for children's behavior are also more frequent, indicating the greater participation on the part of the lovers in the direct dealing with the children. The women in turn feel freer to voice their own opinions. As the living situation continues, the sharing becomes more total, and the ties of family member to family member become more balanced.

It remains to be seen whether within this reconstituted family the redesigned roles of parental involvement and responsibility, based on the new emotional growth of the fathers and the consciousness of women as independent individuals with their own rights and priorities, can be maintained when they run counter to the expected family functioning. It may be that the drastic reduction of the responsibilities on the part of the woman for the maintenance of the family unit and the increased involvement of the father are necessary preconditions for the development of a truly egalitarian or symmetrical marriage. It will also be interesting to see whether these innovative roles can be maintained when the couple begin to have children of their own, in addition to the father's previous offspring.

CHAPTER 7

Conclusion: The Future of the Family

The family is society in embryo: it is the native soil on which performance of moral duty is made easy through natural affection so that within a small circle a basis of moral practice is created and this is later widened to include human relationships in general.

I Ching: The Chinese Book of Changes

. . . indifference to the needs of the young has become one of the distinguishing characteristics of a society that lives for the moment, defines the consumption of commodities as the highest form of personal satisfaction, and exploits existing resources with criminal disregard for the future.

Christopher Lasch in the preface
to *Haven in a Heartless World*

To understand and judge society one has to penetrate its basic structure to the human bond upon which it is built.

Maurice Merleau-Ponty

In the preceding chapters we have presented an example of one such human bond, that between a father and his small child, based on love and need. Our interests go beyond that particular configuration of father and child. We are concerned with the entire parenting relationship. We know that children need parents; we have also argued that parents need their children; and we now want to extend that argument to say that a society needs good parenting relationships.

Parenting as a model of social relationships is of particular interest to us as social scientists concerned with the quality of the social bonds which characterize our interactions. In our society how do the powerful deal with the powerless? How do the knowledgeable deal with the ignorant? How do those who have an easy access to the resources they need for physical and psychological survival treat others who experience more difficulty in making their way to share these resources with those who will come after us, our children and our children's children?

The parenting experience is the most natural model we have available in our culture for these pervasive social relationships. We expect good parents to use all the power, knowledge and resources at their disposal to assist their children's development and to take care of their children's needs. The parental resources, concern and protection are extended until the dependent offspring has developed to his or her fullest potential. Here, power is used not to dominate, but in the service of a weaker individual. Surely, this is a positive model of a humane society.

An alternative model based on exploitation and exclusion of those seen as weaker or less able, has been described and decried in many recent writings. The two that are especially relevant are Christopher Lasch's *The Culture of Narcissism* and Herbert Hendin's *The Age of Sensation*. Both these authors graphically describe a trend towards an alienation of individuals, a fear of commitment to others, and a resultant reluctance to become involved in setting up and maintaining a family. Indeed much of the training that all of us receive for getting ahead in the world of work supports this overly individualized way of functioning.

Although training for independence, self-assertiveness and authoritativeness has recently been explicitly offered to women entering the work world, it has always been the implicit expectation of appropriately socialized males. Male children are expected to distance from the "female" world of mother and develop the "masculine" value of achievement and independence. This task is made difficult for boys whose fathers have been unavailable or emotionally inaccessible to them. For these youths either an exaggerated stereotyped masculinity is learned and reinforced, first by the peer group and later by the competitive world of work (Biller and Meredith, 1974) or masculinity is underdeveloped (Von Franz, 1972). Without a positive paternal relationship to encourage a balanced masculine development, boys can fall pray to either extreme.

Men whose identity is based on the ability to be independent, authoritative and assertive may find that all their relationships follow a negotiation model where two persons cooperate because of a mutual interest. Here, relationships are developed according to how each will contribute to mutual goals. To such negotiations dependency is viewed as a disadvantage since the individual whose needs are greater, or who is less able to make or enforce demands, may not be able to get his or her fair share. Although this model is a characterization of the employer-employee relationship, and even may apply to friends and marriage partners, it is not an ideal model for the relationship between father and child.

A parental relationship is quite different. The child depends on the parent for basic survival. A good parent does not exploit that dependency but accepts and understands it. The child is loved and respected because of the biological and emotional bond between them. Ideally the child should not have to struggle either to get acceptance or care from the parents but expects that they will take his or her interest as their own. The parent hopes to teach his or her children to communicate their needs in an effective way and to begin to take care of themselves. But neither the communication skills, nor self-sufficiency should be preconditions for parental love and acceptance. In other words, parents accept their children's dependency, respond to their needs and support their children in their efforts to reach adulthood and autonomy.

An examination of the parenting relationship can lead us to a better understanding of the following three issues: the definition of the family in its most universal and central aspect, the importance of family participation for adults as well as children, and the effects of divorce both on the structure and the function of a parenting family.

What is a family?

Most of us would feel that we know the answer intuitively; only sociologists, psychologists and anthropologists have difficulty in arriving at a precise definition. We can all agree that a family is a group of people who are related to each other either through marriage or through blood ties. Beyond these ties, how do the individuals in this group act towards each other, and what responsibilities or obligations do they maintain? How the family functions may vary widely from place to place and from time to time. What is it, then, that persists over the varying structures and the varying function which we continue to call family?

There was a time when family members provided for each other all that was necessary for survival and growth: health care, education, food supply, protection, affection, recreation and social status. Many of these functions, at least in their more formal or serious form, have been transferred to outside experts. Education, health care, even entertainment and protection, to name just a few, are only minimally provided by the family group. Rather than being a source of these services, the family in our own society is most likely to be the intermediary through which these services are provided for its individual members.

This tells us what families do but it still does not tell us what they are. One of the major theories in the area of family looks at the relationship between what a family is and what a family does as completely interrelated. This is called structure-function theory and its main proponent has been Talcott Parsons. This theory views what a family is—that is, who it is composed of, where the members live and how it is structured—as a necessary outcome of what it does. What it does is seen as a reflection of what is needed by the larger society. The structural function-alists consider the given form and function of the family to be the best possible adjustment to the requirements of the society at that time. Writing in the 1950s, Parsons found the two-parent family, living in comparative isolation from any extended kin, to be the prevalent family form and argued that such a family is best adjusted for preparing new members to fit their future occupational and family tasks. Parsons expected this family form to perpetuate itself and reinforce the roles of mother and father. This theory has been criticized for its static approach to the notion of family structure and family function, yet it is not certain that this particular criticism would have been made if the events of the following decade had not revealed the instability of the nuclear family.

Since the structural functionalists insisted that the two-parent family was not only the best situation but necessary for the positive development of children, deviations from that form were for a long time looked upon as detrimental to such development. The major focus of research of the 1960s was an attempt to identify the developmental deficits which resulted from family disruption. The orientation was to look for what might be wrong with adults who divorced, and what harm had been incurred by the children of divorcing couples.

We would like to suggest an alternative approach and one which we believe to be more appropriate for analyzing the family as a dynamic and evolving institution. It begins with an attempt to identify the important functions of the family both in terms of child rearing and stabilizing adult roles, and to explore the ways in which these functions continue to be performed under the changing conditions brought about by divorce and other family changes. To do this, we propose that the core concept of family life—the keystone of the kinship system—is not marriage, the institution so considered by Parsons and others, but the parent-child bond. We can then examine the family system to see how the parenting bonds are maintained irrespective of the marital relationship.

This means that we are labeling as a family any grouping of adults who are parents or in a parent-like relationship to a child or children, whether these be never-married mothers, single parents after divorce, or grandparents taking care of their grandchildren. The adults must assume responsibility for the children and have a permanent connection to them. The single parent family, then, is no longer to be viewed as a broken family, but is, in fact, the smallest possible family unit. By the same token, a childless married couple has somewhat less than family status. The bond between these two partners may or may not be permanent. In other words, a "family" of two adults lacks the universal and permanent features which characterize a parent-child unit.

This refocusing of the central family bond from one between two adults to one between adults and children has the additional consequence of de-emphasizing the ties between the family system and occupational system which Parsons so strongly emphasized. We cannot deny that flexibility of time as well as a certain amount of material comfort may relate directly to participation in family life. Most of our respondents mention some work flexibility as a basic necessity for extended parenting, but this is not always a necessary requirement. In our study of married fathers, we have seen that time fathers spend with children is uncorrelated with work involvement. Some part-time workers spend little of their nonwork time caring for their children, while other fathers who report working more than full-time still are the ones who make breakfast for their children, send them off to school, make dinners and read them bedtime stories. It appears that parenting time for married men is an expression of priorities and decisions about the desired level of participation. This is also true for single parents, mothers and fathers alike, who find many different ways of integrating their child-care time with work obligations (Weiss, 1978).

Before we discuss other aspects of the parent-child bond as the core concept for understanding family structure, we want to examine briefly one other theory of the family. The progressivist theory of the family has been credited to William F. Ogburn as expressed in his book *Technology and the Changing Family*. He viewed the family as adjusting to changing historical forces which act upon it from the outside. Although his analysis referred mainly to technological change, he viewed the material changes imposed by technological progress as having consequences for the nonmaterial or value aspects of family life. The family, pressured by the changing environment, tends to lag behind the cultural progress, and it is this lag, according to Ogburn, that accounts in large measure for the difficulties families encounter and the disorganization they suffer. Although his analysis has much in common with the excellent cross-cultural studies of William Goode on the effects of industrialization and urbanization on families, Ogburn confines his discussion to the American family and does not consider the ways in which families might resist such external pressures.

According to Ogburn, when the family ceased to be a produtive unit the members were freed to attend more to their emotional lives. Thus, although the family has fewer functions today than in the past, it may be that these functions, largely confined to the affective area, are performed better. The importance of Ogburn's writing at the time it appeared was to call attention to the impact of technology on social change and to criticize governmental interference in family life.

We can reexamine Ogburn's notions in our terms by tracing throughout his descriptions of the family both the changing concepts of the developmental needs of children as they were affected by the psychological and pedagogical theories of the day, and the changes in parental consciousness as the specific responsibilities and expectations of parents changed with the altered social situation.

The current changes in the roles of men and women make it appropriate to consider their family roles in parallel ways. The major emphasis given to occupational structures in theories of the family has been suspect when mothers were so often the child rearers and were not expected to participate in the labor market. It is even more suspect with the increased participation of men in child rearing and involvement in child-care structures such as play groups, parent-child conferences, babysitting and informal meetings with other parents, all of which were once the province of mothers. Such involvements make individual parents more directly responsive to their families and less to the demands of their jobs.

The current changes in the family roles of men and women do not represent a direct adjustment to occupational or technological demands. They are an expression of the conceptualization of human needs as exemplified by the new expectations of women and the changing possibility of the development of parental involvement by both sexes. As these new expectations continue to heighten the visibility of the conflicting demands of work and family, many individuals choose not to become parents. We consider this a definite loss to the adults themselves and to society as a whole. The raising of children requires direct inputs of time and energy into the parent-child relationship. Ideally participation in the family, in turn, resocializes the adults into more responsive, empathetic and socially responsible persons through developing their parental consciousness. Parental consciousness is the adults' understanding of the needs of children and their willingness and ability to perceive those needs and respond to them appropriately. Whereas a focus on occupational status in analyzing family structure assumes that the family has to adjust to the demands of the work world, a focus on parental consciousness brings to our attention the conflicts between the needs of the family and the other demands made on working adults by the outside world.

Parental Consciousness

We make the assumption that even when the child's basic survival needs for shelter and food are met by institutional means, from a boarding school to a kibbutz or other collective caretaking situation, there still remains an important part of caretaking which involves giving love, acceptance and providing adult models for behavior. These latter functions, central to parenting, must be performed by an adult who has a unique connection to the child. It is of utmost psychological importance that there be available to each child at least one adult, and preferably more than one, who is perceived as permanently related and legitimately obligated to be the child's caretakers. It is imperative for the eventual development of self-esteem and fostering of identification that the child have the right to the time and attention of specific adults. When we speak of parents, then, we do not mean only or necessarily biological parents, but also other adults who accept the obligation to respond to the needs of the child.

There are three characteristics that comprise parental consciousness:

(a) availability,
(b) accessibility and
(c) responsiveness.

(a) Availability refers to physical presence both in actual time spent with the child and the time spent on call in case a need arises. Available parents think of themselves in terms of their parental responsibility. In practical terms it means being reachable by phone and arriving on time when child-care arrangements end. It means understanding the right of the child to the parent's time. This dimension is one that many fathers find a difficult adjustment when they parent after divorce. Most men expect to give their time to their work as a clear priority. In two-parent families, such time is often given unconditional respect. "Daddy can't do . . . because he has to go to work," allows no dispute. But men who parent alone find that this is no longer the case. When conflict arises between time they must give to their children, whether it is waiting with their small child for a school bus which is late, or sitting in the doctor's waiting room, or being interrupted at work by a phone call from home, each instance must now be considered on its own merit. Important events in the child's life, from emergencies to simply a few moments of sharing a small triumph or a thought, now may take priority over the previously immutable work time. Since the child expects the parent to be there for him or her and the parent wishes to live up to that expectation, availability becomes a real daily issue and a point of struggle among the many demands on the parents' time and attention.

(b) Accessibility. It is not enough to make one's time available to the child. One must also be emotionally accessible, "really there" for an interaction to be meaningful. In the past, accessibility has been the province of mothers, compared to the prevalent description of fathers as "remote" in studies of parental relationships (Komarovsky, 1976). We are familiar with the caricatured image of the father who hidden behind the newspaper, nods his head absentmindedly at the child's accounts, forgets birthdays and seems to know little about children. However, once the marriage breaks up, such remote fathers must emerge from behind the newspaper or whatever barrier has kept them from direct parenting, in order to maintain a place in their children's lives. To learn how to be accessible means to allow the child into the inner space of the adult attention. It means to take the contents of the child's life seriously and accept them for whatever importance they have in the child's own view. It means a willingness to structure certain aspects of the adult life on the child's level, whether it is sharing a trip or a movie, listening to jokes that are only funny to six-year-olds, changing mealtimes to accommodate an early bedtime, or simplifying menus. In summary, it means allowing a certain part of the adult's life to be restructured by the needs of the child. A consequence of the parent's accessibility is the possibility of a genuine exchange between parent and child. One father of a six-year-old was chastened when his son brought a drawing home to show him and, after hearing the perfunctory "That's very good, dear," replied "You don't have to say that, Dad, I didn't do it." Another father put it this way, "Now that the kids are with me and Jill tells me about her day, I don't just nod and say 'how nice,' I really have to talk to her." Having to "really talk" to one's children means really getting to know them.

(c) Responsiveness. Getting to know one's children opens the way to responding to them as unique and special individuals. Responsiveness is the quality which binds together a series of parent-child interactions into a relationship which can grow in breadth and depth. It is the concrete expression of a parent's love, understanding and appreciation of his or her child. It is his or her way of letting the child experience the special bond and attachment between them. It requires careful paying of attention and communicates concern.

John, a rather serious father in our study, expressed his responsiveness to four-year-old Melissa when he stopped telling her there were no monsters in her room and frightened the monsters away with a loud yell. Another father described his responsiveness in the following way:

At first, Joey seemed to be following me around all the time and I kept telling him to play in his room. Finally I realized that he was fearful when I was out of sight. I stopped pushing him and learned to live with my little shadow.

Parental responsiveness heightens the unique connection between parent and child and promotes the identification between them. If a child is to identify with a parent in a way that will promote his or her development as a unique individual with a strong sense of self, that child must see his or her uniqueness reflected in the parent's response. The reward for developing responsiveness is the enjoyment of the child as special and important to the parent, and the improvement of relational skills for the parent in his or her own adult interactions.

One of the major effects of parenting experience for men is the necessity to give up some of their independence in order to form close relationships. Robert Weiss (1979), in discussing the benefits of single parenting, quotes the following:

Six months ago my sixteen-year-old daughter came to live with me . . . It had a startling effect on me. Having another person in the house, creating a home again, the responsibility of having a child, someone depending on me a little bit, it gave me a feeling of having more purpose in life, that I was not there all alone, that I was really a parent again, that I had the responsibility and someone was dependent on me. It was a kind of reawakening type of thing. It changed an apartment into a home, almost. I always saw the children a lot, but having her live with me, it shook me a little bit to realize the change in my outlook that this brought (p. 254-260).

This is often a new insight for men who have been taught to value standing alone and being self-sufficient. Seeing their children in need, being able to meet those needs and seeing themselves change through that interaction, bring a new understanding of growth through interdependence. The need for others and the bonds that are forged because of the child's dependency can be seen as sustaining to a relationship and enhancing for the father's own sense of himself.

These are the parenting adjustments that are usually more difficult for men than they are for women. Women are expected to be dependent, to need help, and to give time and energy to nurturance. Through the process of birth women experience the interdependence that sustains human life and the full vulnerability of the newborn. Men achieve their adulthood by leaving behind the dependency of their growing years. Their adulthood is conferred upon them by the wider social world of work. Erving Goffman says in his book *Asylums:* "Our sense of being a person can come from being drawn into a wider social unit: our sense of selfhood can come from the little ways in which we resist the pull." (p. 386.)

There are many reasons structured into the lives of women, sometimes too many, which give them the opportunity or the necessity to resist the pull. There are few opportunities for most men to resist the pull of the work world. The father in our sample, who after describing the changes he had undergone as a divorced parent, concluded by saying "I always wanted to be like that but never had an excuse to," was expressing just this sentiment. He had become more home oriented, more giving, less concerned with making money or achieving prestige. His new involvement in child care allowed him to resist the pull of the wider society.

We expect that when the job of caring and nurturing through the parenting experience becomes the legitimate function of men, their understanding of the importance of interdependence for human survival will affect their participation in the wider society as well.

The more the fathers spent time with children the more they spoke of profound personal changes:

"I have slowed down."
"I am more home oriented and more tuned in to others."
"It's easier for me to express emotions."
"I like myself better."

"I have learned to communicate better and I have more fun."
"I am more myself."
"I think I just feel more a part of humanity than I did before I took care of my children."

These are some typical responses. Ninety-seven percent of the fathers gave some response to the question about the effect of child care that fell into the category "personal growth." Becoming more responsible, more self-reliant, stable and relaxed were also frequent results.

On the negative side, most men complained of lack of time for themselves and for adult social activities. It is difficult, even impossible at times, to raise children without some assistance from others. This brings an additional motivation for cooperation and coexistence with others. Cooperative living, extended family arrangements and other forms of sharing become appealing alternatives to the nuclear family. Thus what is meant by parental consciousness is not only the emotional and practical education around the performance of child-care tasks, but a more generalized awareness of the necessary interdependence and responsibility for others which are important characteristics of a caring and humane society.

The Postdivorce Family Structure

Theorists of the family have recognized a great variety of family forms. Besides the nuclear families there are polygamous families, in some of which children acknowledge more than one mother, and extended families where a grandparent is viewed as the head of the family and does most of the decision making. There are families where only brothers live together and others where siblings and cousins of both sexes are barely distinguishable. The frequency of divorce in our own culture and the ability of a single parent and child to maintain themselves economically and to live in a separate household has given rise to a new kind of family: the postdivorce, multi-residence family. This family occupies more than one household, and yet shares a common interest in the common children.

One of the most striking findings emerging from our interview material was the persistence of family connections between both parents and children following divorce. This was not just a matter of love or family feelings. Family functions included financial support, practical assistance, decisions about health and education. The more our respondents were able to preserve and protect many of these family functions, the more satisfied they felt with their lives and with themselves.

Regardless of their legal status, these individuals still constituted a family by most criteria. This made it clear to us that the keystone of family structure is parenthood. Moreover, the obligations of parenthood cannot be legally dissolved, and the configuration of parents and children remains a family even after divorce and remarriage. That marriage partners can divorce need not require that a parent divorces his or her children.

The essential element of the postdivorce family is the strengthening of the relationships between each parent and each child, between siblings and between the divorced spouses in respect to the welfare of their offspring. To develop, insure and encourage these relationships during the difficult process of divorce, a new commitment by the legal system, by public and private mental health institutions and by the occupational sector is needed. Presently, with few exceptions, these institutions often covertly encourage single parenting rather than shared parenting. Divorcing spouses wishing to develop a cooperative parenting arrangement too often must act against the efforts of lawyers, mental health therapists and judges who declare that such ''new ideas'' are unsound, unwise and detrimental to children. Yet, the latest research data shows that children develop positively and are eased in their emotional and social adjustments to parental divorce when both parents cooperate in their care on a consistent and continued basis (Wallerstein and Kelly, 1979).

Rather than viewing divorce as family breakdown, we recognize divorce as a process of restructuring of the nuclear family toward a new form which, when possible, supports shared parenting. During the past four years, one of the authors, Harry Keshet, and other members of the Divorce Resource and Mediation Center, Inc., in Cambridge, Massachusetts have developed the following guidelines for negotiating a new family structure with divorcing spouses.* When negotiations lead to agreements between spouses, they are often incorporated into the legal divorce settlement and, if accepted by the courts, given legal support for shared parenting. The guidelines include four elements: custody, decision making, the residence of children, and dealing with conflicts and change.

WHO HAS CUSTODY? Custody of children is shared and it is the right and responsibility of both parents to participate in the rearing of their children. Neither parent has more rights than the other. Custody rests squarely with both parents.

SHARED DECISION MAKING. Decisions concerning the children's education, medical care and religious training are jointly made by both parents. One parent cannot act unilaterally nor does one parent have the full burden of decision making. Since parenting requires the right of participation in the major decision-making areas of the growing child's life, this provision also includes the right of access to information and participation in the child-serving institutions in order to make sound decisions. Access includes the right of both parents to meet with personnel, see records and receive information from schools, hospitals, day-care centers, and religious institutions serving their children. Neither parent can be excluded from participation with these institutions.

WHERE DO CHILDREN LIVE? Determination of the residence of children and time periods spent with each parent requires careful examination by parents, children and helping professionals. Shared parenting does not require specific time periods such as half-time or quarter-time residence. Each situation is unique and depends on the age of the child, physical proximity of ex-spouse

---

*The Divorce Resource and Mediation Center, Incorporated, is a nonprofit mental health facility offering family counseling and divorce mediation. Special recognition for contributing to the development of these guidelines is given Jamie Keshet, Larry Madfis, and Jerry Weinstein.

households, parenting abilities, parent-child attachments and the ability of parents to cooperate in shared parenting. Besides establishing regular child-care schedules and residence, holiday and vacation agreements are helpful.

We have found that specifying where children will spend their holidays and vacations, where and at what times they will be picked up and returned, helps the divorcing family with creating their new structure. Holidays and vacations are family times and parents and children often need help in negotiating the details of a new family arrangement so often colored by past memories, images and fears of loss and exclusion.

DEALING WITH CONFLICT AND CHANGE. Shared parenting often generates hostile conflicts between parents. After all, are not the inability to make mutual decisions or marked difference in perspective or values among the reasons why people separate? Conflict cannot be eliminated but conflict need not mean that the divorcing couples, even with past failures and different perspectives, cannot cooperate for the benefit of their children. We have found at the Divorce Resource and Mediation Center that spouses locked in rancorous conflict over their marital relationship are able to cooperate concerning their children. As noted in previous chapters, a necessary element in securing cooperation is the separation of the role of spouse from the role of parent. When this division is achieved, shared parenting is facilitated.

Parents can create a mechanism for helping with this role separation and with conflict management by agreeing to mediate their differences. A specific person, usually a mental health professional familiar with child development, can be named in the agreement to work with the family during and after the divorce on a continuing basis. The mediator also helps the family negotiate changes in their agreements as new situations develop for individual family members or between members. Such changes include geographic and occupational mobility, issues of children's maturation, remarriage of a spouse, and negotiating roles of new family members (lovers, stepparents, stepchildren). Mediation allows for the reality that the postdivorce family structure must be dynamic and have the mechanism to deal with change. Just as change is expected in nuclear families as children and parents mature, change in the shared parenting structure must be accepted as normal. For example, the weekend child-care schedule that was positive for the grade school child needing security may be a hindrance for the teenager needing independence. The shared parenting family must expect change not as a reflection of poor decisions of the past but rather as a reflection of the need for the family system to adjust to developmental and environmental demands.

We are not suggesting that all families should or need to adopt a shared parenting family structure. Certainly there are examples where one or both parents may be psychologically or emotionally unfit to parent. We are suggesting that shared parenting be a serious alternative among existing postdivorce family arrangements. It is our belief that many children, parents and extended family members have suffered needlessly because of rigid beliefs and untested assumptions concerning the best interests of children.

Support for postdivorce families must consist of the recognition by the legal system, public agencies and other institutions which deal with children and the family of the continued rights and obligations of both parents after a marital separation. Such recognition is slowly becoming legitimized through the introduction of shared parenting arrangements, increased access to children by fathers and the increased publicity about parenting by fathers. The reality of the lives of the children of divorce, the fact that their names may differ from that of their mothers, that they may have two homes, that some of their time is spent away from their neighborhoods, all these considerations must be part of educational and child-care planning.

For the parenting fathers themselves, this support must be obtained in three areas: personal acceptance by extended family members, friends and coworkers; job structures and achievement expectations which support parenting; and child-oriented situations which are supportive of fathers.

Acceptance by others is the most frequent request of the fathers we interviewed when asked about changes they would like to see. Although most men are able to get some support for their parenting from women friends, from their ex-wives and other peers, they must often withstand the disapproval and scepticism of their own parents and other members of the extended family. Dire predictions about the unfortunate effects of child care both on the father and the children have to be withstood and add to the existing burdens of readjustment. Hopefully as more and more fathers do live with their children and parent alone these situations will cease to seem an oddity.

Acceptance at work has very real, practical consequences for the fathers. Being able to accept phone calls from children at work, having some time flexibility for the inevitable family emergencies that arise, or even just being able to express the concerns or pleasures of parenthood to coworkers are important aspects of the work environment. The standard assumption is that men will give their priority in time and energy to their jobs. Parenting fathers who may wish to alter these priorities may experience discrimination in the work place (George and Wilding, 1973; Keshet and Rosenthal, 1976).

Finally, acceptance of the legitimacy of fathers as parents in settings where children are being cared for—schools, agencies, and health care institutions—is an important validation of their parenting role. Among our respondents one father had been refused access to the child's teacher with whom he wished to discuss a classroom problem because he was not the custodial parent. He was told by the principal that he could talk to the teacher generally about the class but was not entitled to information about his son. Another father was asked, when he accompanied his child to the dentist, to have the mother call for hygiene information. When he objected, he was told it was "better" according to the doctor to talk to the mother. Parenting by fathers also becomes a challenge and an adventure in more informal settings—birthday parties where other youngsters are accompanied by their mothers, calling a teenage babysitter whose mother may be wary of allowing her daughter to come to the house of a "single" man, and all the myriad other unpredictable child-care situations which heretofore have been the province of mothers. We cannot disagree that it is often a struggle, but feel it is more than compensated for by its rewards.

The awareness of the increasing numbers of men who parent and the conscious support of such parenting must lead to an extension of family support services to fathers as well as mothers. Agencies must acquaint themselves with the practical and psychological problems of parenting men and extend their services to deal with this population.

Agencies must also acquaint themselves with the two-household child who has two emergency phone numbers and who may be accompanied for service by either parent or stepparent. They must be familiar with children who are available for after-school programs only on Mondays, Tuesdays, and Wednesdays but not on Thursdays and Fridays when they go to their other parent's home. They must add to their old image of divorced children as being neglected, abandoned and deprived of enough parental affection and care to include the child with two active biological parents, two sets of stepparents, siblings, stepsiblings, half-siblings, grandparents and stepgrandparents. They must become prepared to understand, appreciate and assist in the complexity and richness of the emerging multi-residence postdivorce family structures.

Self and Typical Male Rating Scale*

1 Never or almost never true   5 Often true

2 Usually not true   6 Usually true

3 Sometimes but infrequently true   7 Always or almost always true

4 Occasionally true

_____Self Reliant

_____Yielding

_____Helpful

_____Defends own
    beliefs

_____Cheerful

_____Moody

_____Independent

_____Shy

_____Conscientious

_____Athletic

_____Affectionate

_____Theatrical

_____Assertive

_____Flatterable

_____Happy

_____Strong
    personality

_____Loyal

_____Unpredictable

_____Forceful

_____Feminine

_____Reliable

_____Analytical

_____Sympathetic

_____Jealous

_____Has leadership
    abilities

_____Sensitive to the
    needs of
    others

_____Truthful

_____Willing to take
    risks

_____Understanding

_____Secretive

_____Makes
    decisions
    easily

_____Compassionate

_____Sincere

_____Self-Sufficient

_____Eager to soothe
    hurt feelings

_____Conceited

_____Dominant

_____Soft-spoken

_____Likable

_____Masculine

_____Warm

_____Solemn

_____Willing to take
    a stand

_____Tender

_____Friendly

_____Aggressive

_____Gullible

_____Inefficient

_____Acts as a leader

_____Childlike

_____Adaptable

_____Individualistic

_____Does not use
    harsh
    language

_____Unsystematic

_____Competitive

_____Loves children

_____Tactful

_____Ambitious

_____Gentle

_____Conventional

*Modified from Beim (1974) "The Measurement of psychological andro-gyne," *Journal of Consulting and Clinical Psych.*, 1974, *42*, 155–162.

APPENDIX B

TABLE 1   RELATIONS WITH EX-WIFE BY LEVEL OF CHILD CARE

Level of Child Care	Friendly N	Friendly %	Somewhat Friendly N	Somewhat Friendly %	Distant N	Distant %	Total N	Total %
Less than Quarter time	6	21	7	24	15	55	28	100
Quarter time	6	28	10	48	5	24	21	100
Half time	6	21	16	55	7	24	29	100
Full time	10	20	17	36	22	44	49	100

TABLE 2   FREQUENCY OF COMMUNICATION WITH EX-WIFE BY LEVEL OF CHILD CARE

Level of Child Care	Daily N	Daily %	Weekly N	Weekly %	Monthly N	Monthly %	Rarely N	Rarely %	Total N	Total %
Less than Quarter time	5	17	20	72	2	7	1	4	28	100
Quarter time	4	19	16	76	1	5	0	0	21	100
Half time	5	17	22	76	2	7	0	0	29	100
Full time	5	10	33	48	4	9	16	33	48	100

TABLE 3   WHO INITIATES CONTACT BY LEVEL OF CHILD CARE

Level of Child Care	Self N	Self %	Wife N	Wife %	Both N	Both %	Other N	Other %	Total N	Total %
Less than Quarter time	10	36	4	14	12	43	2	7	28	100
Quarter time	12	56	2	10	7	33	0	0	21	100
Half time	7	25	6	21	15	54	0	0	28	100
Full time	13	27	14	39	13	27	3	6	48	100

TABLE 4   HOW IS EX-WIFE AS A PARENT BY LEVEL OF CHILD CARE

Level of Child Care	Excellent/ Good		Adequate		Inadequate		Total	
	N	%	N	%	N	%	N	%
Less than Quarter time	18	70	4	15	4	15	26	100
Quarter time	16	76	3	14	2	10	21	100
Half time	27	94	1	3	1	3	29	100
Full time	11	22	11	22	27	56	49	100

TABLE 5   CHARACTERISTICS USED TO DESCRIBE EX-WIFE BY LEVEL OF CHILD CARE

Level of Child Care	Positive		Negative		Neutral		Total	
	N	%	N	%	N	%	N	%
Less than Quarter time	7	25	16	57	5	18	28	100
Quarter time	13	63	5	23	3	14	21	100
Half time	21	72	5	18	3	10	29	100
Full time	21	43	26	53	2	4	49	100

TABLE 6   SOCIAL CONTACT WITH EX-SPOUSE BY LEVEL OF CHILD CARE

Level of Child Care	Occasion- ally		Regu- larly		Fre- quently		Never		Total	
	N	%	N	%	N	%	N	%	N	%
Less than Quarter time	7	26	1	4	3	11	16	59	27	100
Quarter time	6	29	4	19	1	5	10	47	21	100
Half time	5	17	5	17	1	4	18	62	29	100
Full time	6	13	10	22	–	–	30	65	46	100

TABLE 7   DISCUSS PERSONAL PROBLEMS WITH EX-WIFE BY LEVEL OF
CHILD CARE

Level of Child Care	Yes N	%	No N	%	Total N	%
Less than						
Quarter time	15	54	13	46	28	100
Quarter time	12	60	8	40	20	100
Half time	9	31	20	69	29	100
Full time	15	33	30	63	45	100

TABLE 8   FATHER'S INCOME BY LEVEL OF CHILD CARE

Level of Child Care	Less than $5000 N	%	$5000 to $9999 N	%	$10,000 to $14,999 N	%	$15,000 to $19,999 N	%	$20,000 to $24,999 N	%	$25,000 and above N	%	Total N	%
Less than														
Quarter time	2	7	7	25	5	18	2	7	5	18	7	25	28	100
Quarter time	3	14	4	19	0	0	3	14	6	29	5	24	21	100
Half time	4	14	3	10	5	21	7	24	4	14	3	17	29	100
Full Time	7	15	7	16	14	30	6	14	5	10	7	15	46	100

Works Cited in the Text

Allen, William P. "Marital Fidelity." *Journal of Marriage and the Family* (Winter 1965): 273–301.

Ariès, Philippe. *Centuries of Childhood*. New York: Jonathan Cape, 1962.

Atkin, Edith, and Rubin, Estelle. *Part-Time Father*. New York: Signet Books, 1977.

Bell, Norman, and Vogel, Ezra F. *A Modern Introduction to the Family*. Rev. ed. New York: Free Press, 1968.

Benson, Leonard. *Fathering: A Sociological Perspective*. New York: Random House, 1968.

Bettelheim, Bruno. *Symbolic Wounds*. New York: Collier Books, 1962.

Bigner, Jerry J. "Fathering: Research and Practical Implications." *Family Coordinator* 19 (October 1970): 357–62.

Biller, Henry, and Meredith, Donald. *Father Power*. New York: David McKay, 1974.

Blau, Peter M. *The Dynamics of Bureaucracy*. Chicago: University of Chicago Press, 1955.

Blau, Peter M. *Exchange and Power in Social Life*. New York: John Wiley & Sons, 1964.

Blau, Peter M., and Duncan, O. Dudley. *The American Occupational Structure*. New York: John Wiley & Sons, 1967.

Bogue, Donald. *Population of the United States*. Glencoe, Ill.: Free Press, 1949.

Bohannan, Paul. *Divorce and After*. New York: Doubleday, 1970.

Bowlby, John. *Maternal Care and Mental Health*. Geneva: World Health Organization, 1951.

Brenton, Myron. *The American Male*. New York: Fawcett, 1966.

Brown, Carol A.; Feldberg, Rosalind; Fox, Elizabeth M.; and Kohn, Janet. "Divorce: Chance of a New Lifetime." *Journal of Social Issues* 32 (Winter 1976): 119–33.

Cox, Frank D. *Human Intimacy: Marriage, the Family and Its Meaning*. St. Paul: West, 1978.

Emerson, Robert M. "Power Dependence Relations." *American Sociological Review* 27 (February 1962): 31–41.

Erikson, Erik. *Youth, Identity and Crisis*. New York: W. W. Norton, 1968.

Fisher, Esther O. "A Guide to Divorce Counseling." *Family Coordinator* 22 (January 1973): 55–61.

Fox, David, and Steinman, Anne. *The Male Dilemma*. New York: Harper & Row, 1974.

George, Victor, and Wilding, Paul. *Motherless Families*. London: Routledge & Kegan Paul, 1973.

Glick, Paul C. "Some Recent Changes in American Families." *Current Population Reports*, Series P-23, No. 52. U.S. Bureau of the Census. Washington, D.C.: Government Printing Office, 1975.

Glick, Paul C., and Norton, Arthur J. "Marrying, Divorcing, and Living Together in the U.S. Today." *Population Bulletin* 32 (October 1977): 3–39.

Goffman, Erving. *Asylums*. New York: Anchor Books, 1961.

Goldstein, Joseph; Freud, Anna; and Solnit, Albert J. *Beyond the Best Interests of the Child*. New York: Free Press, 1973.

Goode, William J. *After Divorce*. New York: Free Press, 1956.

Gordon, Michael. *The American Family*. New York: Random House, 1978.

Harlow, Harry F., and Harlow, Margaret K. "Learning to Love." *American Scientist* 54 (1966): 244–72.

Harlow, Harry F., and Zimmerman, Robert. "Affectional Responses in the Infant Monkey." *Science* 130 (1959): 421–32.

Henry, Jules. *Culture Against Man*. New York: Random House, 1963.

Hess, Robert, and Shipman, Victor. "Early Experience and the Socialization of Cognitive Modes in Children." *Child Development* 36 (December 1965): 869–86.

Holmstrom, Lynda L. *The Two-Career Marriage*. Cambridge, Mass.: Schenkman, 1972.

Hunt, Morton. *The World of the Formerly Married*. New York: McGraw-Hill, 1966.

Kemper, Theodore D. "Power, Status, and Love." In *Personality and Socialization*, edited by David R. Heise. Chicago: Rand McNally, 1972.

Keshet, Harry, and Rosenthal, Kristine. "Fathering after Marital Separation." *Social Work* 23 (January 1977): 11–18.

Keshet, Harry, and Rosenthal, Kristine. "Not Quite Stepmothers: Women in the Lives of Divorced Fathers." *Psychology Today* 12 (1978): 74–80.

Komarovsky, Mirra. *Dilemmas of Masculinity*. New York: W. W. Norton, 1976.

Kotelchuck, Milton. "The Nature of the Infant's Tie to his Father." Paper presented at the annual meeting of the Society for Research in Child Development, Philadelphia, April 1973.

Le Masters, E. E. *Parents in Modern America*. Homewood, Ill.: Dorsey Press, 1974.

Levine, James A. *Who Will Raise the Children? New Options for Fathers (and Mothers)*. New York: Bantam Books, 1977.

Lynn, David. *The Father: His Role in Child Development*. Monterey: Brooks/Cole, 1974.

Mead, Margaret. *Male and Female*. New York: Dell, 1953.

Mead, Margaret. *The Family*. New York: Macmillan, 1965.

Miller, Daniel R., and Swanson, Guy E. *The Changing American Parent*. New York: John Wiley & Sons, 1958.

Mitchell, George H. *Paternalistic Behavior and Primates*. New York: Holt & Rinehart, 1969.

Morse, Norman C., and Weiss, Robert S. "The Function and Meaning of Work and the Job." *American Sociological Review* 20 (April 1955): 191–98.

Oakley, Ann. *Woman's Work*. New York: Pantheon Books, 1974.

O'Neill, Nora, and O'Neill, George. *Open Marriage*. New York: Avon, 1972.

Parsons, Talcott. *Social Structure and Personality*. New York: Free Press, 1964.

Parsons, Talcott, and Bales, Robert. *Family Socialization and Interaction Process*. New York: Free Press, 1955.

Pleck, Joseph. "Work and Family Roles: From Sex-Patterned Segregation to Integration." Paper presented at the Meeting of the American Sociological Association, San Francisco, August, 1975.

Polatnick, Margaret M. "Why Men Don't Rear Children: A Power Analysis." *Berkeley Journal of Sociology* 18 (1973–74): 45–86.

Polema, Margaret M., and Garland, Thomas N. "The Married Professional Woman: A Study in the Tolerance of Domestication." *Journal of Marriage and the Family* 33 (1971): 531–40.

Rainwater, Lee. "Work, Well-Being and Family Life." In *Work and the Quality of Life*, edited by James O'Toole. Cambridge, Mass.: M.I.T. Press, 1974.

Rapoport, Rhona, and Rapoport, Robert. *Dual Career Families*. London: Penguin, 1971.

Reiss, Ira L. "The Universality of the Family: A Conceptual Analysis." *Journal of Marriage and the Family* 27 (November 1960): 443–56.

Roland, Warren L. "Family Maintenance in Father-Only Families." Study Project based at Brandeis University Florence Hiller Graduate School in Waltham, Massachusetts, 1975.

Roy, Robert, and Roy, D. *Honest Sex*. New York: New American Library, 1970.

Rubin, Lillian B. *Worlds of Pain: Life in the Working-Class Family*. New York: Basic Books, 1976.

Seeley, John. *Crestwood Heights*. New York: Basic Books, 1956.

Stack, Carol B. "Who Owns the Child? Divorce and Child Custody Decisions in Middle-Class Families." *Social Problems* 23 (April 1976): 505–15.

Thibaut, John W., and Kelley, Harold A. *The Social Psychology of Groups*. New York: John Wiley & Sons, 1959.

Veroff, Joel, and Feld, Sheila. *Marriage and Work in America*. New York: Van Nostrand Reinhold, 1970.

Von Franz, Marie Louise. *Puer Aternus*. New York, N.Y.: Spring Press, 1972.

Walker, Kenneth N.; Rogers, Joy; and Messinger, Lillian. "Remarriage after Divorce: A Review." *Social Casework* 58 (May 1977): 276–81.

Waller, Willard. *The Old Love and the New*. Carbondale, Ill.: Southern Illinois Press, 1967.

Wallerstein, Judith S., and Kelly, Joan B. "Children and Divorce: A Review." *Social Work* 24 (November 1979: 468–75.

Weiss, Robert S. *Going it Alone: The Family Life and Social Situations of Single Parents*. New York: Basic Books, 1979.

Weiss, Robert S. "Transitional States and Other Stressful Situations." In *Support Systems and Mutual Help,* edited by Leonard Caplan and Mary Killilee. New York: Grune & Stratton, 1976.

Wilensky, Harold L. "Work as a Social Problem." In *Social Problems and Modern Approach,* edited by H. S. Becker. New York: John Wiley & Sons, 1966.

General Bibliography

FATHER ROLE

Bell, Robert. "The Significance of the Father: Some Theoretical and Empirical Considerations." Unpublished paper. Philadelphia: Temple University, 1959.

Benson, Leonard. *Fathering: A Sociological Perspective*. New York: Random House, 1968.

Bigner, Jerry J. "Fathering: Research and Practical Implications." *Family Coordinator* 19 (October 1970): 357–62.

Biller, Henry, and Meredith, Donald. *Father Power*. New York: David McKay, 1974.

Brenton, Myron. "The Paradox of the American Father." In *The Future of the Family*, edited by Louise Howe. New York: Simon & Schuster, 1972.

Broderick, Carol B. "Fathers." *Family Coordinator* 25 (October 1977): 126–32.

Dodson, Fitzhugh. *How to Father*. New York: New American Library, 1974.

Eversoll, Deanra. "A Two Generational View of Fathering." *Family Coordinator* 28 (October 1979): 11–18.

Fein, Robert A. "Research on Fathering: Social Policy and an Emergent Perspective." *The Journal of Social Issues* 34 (Winter 1978): 72–91.

Gilbert, Sara D. *What's a Father for? A Father's Guide to the Pleasures and Problems of Parenthood with Advice from the Experts*. New York: Parents' Magazine Press, 1975.

Howells, John G. "Fallacies in Child Care II: That Fathering is Unimportant." *ACTA Paedopsychiatrica* 37 (1970): 126–32.

Kelman, Herbert. "Social and Psychoanalytic Reflections on the Father." *American Scholar* 29 (1969): 7–8.

Klein, Carole. *The Single Parent Experience.* New York: Walker, 1973.

Klein, Ted. *The Father's Book.* New York: William Morrow, 1968.

Klein, Ted. *Father and Child.* New York: William Morrow, 1968.

LeMasters, E. E. "The Passing of the Dominant Husband-Father." In *Family, Marriage and the Struggle of the Sexes,* edited by Hans P. Dreitzel. New York: Macmillan, 1972.

Levine, James A. *Who Will Raise the Children? New Options for Fathers (and Mothers).* Philadelphia: Lippincott, 1976.

Lewis, Robert A., and Pleck, Joseph H. "Men's Roles in the Family." *Family Coordinator* 28 (October 1970): 21–29.

Lott, Bernice. "Who Wants the Children: Some Relationships Among Attitudes Towards Children, Parents and the Liberation of Women." *American Psychologist* 46 (October 1973): 14–16.

Meerlo, Joast. "The Psychological Role of the Father." *Child and Family* 7 (Spring 1968): 102–16.

Nash, John. "The Father in Contemporary Culture and Current Psychological Literature." *Child Development* 36 (1965): 261–97.

Nash, John. "Father in Contemporary Culture: Father/Son Relationship." *Child Development* 33 (1965): 212–31.

Nye, F. Ivan, and Berardo, Felix M. "Changes in husband and father roles." In *The Family: Its Structure and Interaction,* edited by Kenneth J. Scotte. New York: Macmillan, 1973.

Parke, Robert D., and Savin, David B. "Fathering: It's a Major Role." *Psychology Today* 11 (November 1977): 108–13.

Petras, John W., ed. *Sex: Male/Gender: Masculine.* Washington: Alfred, 1975.

Polatnick, Margaret M. "Why Men Don't Rear Children: A Power Analysis." *Berkeley Journal of Sociology* 18 (1973–74): 45–86.

Price-Bonham, Sharon. "Bibliography of Literature Related to Role of Fathers." *Family Coordinator* 25 (October 1976): 142–46.

Rapoport, Rhona; Rapoport, Robert N.; and Stelitz, S. *Fathers, Mothers and Society: Towards New Alliances.* New York: Basic Books, 1977.

Reynolds, William. *The American Father.* New York: Paddington Press, 1978.

Schulte, S. R. "Role of the Father in the Family." *Clearing House* 46 (March 1972): 140–43.

Tasch, R. J. "The Role of the Father in the Family." *Journal of Experimental Education* 20 (June 1952): 319–61.

FATHERING AND CHILD DEVELOPMENT

Anthony, E. James, and Benedek, Therese, eds. "Fatherhood and Providing." *Parenthood: Its Psychology and Psychopathology.* Boston: Little, Brown, 1970.

Biller, Henry B. "Father Absence and the Personality Development of the Male Child." *Developmental Psychology* 2 (March 1970): 181–201.

Biller, Henry B. *Father, Child, and Sex Role*. Lexington: Heath, 1974.

Earles, F. Anthony. "Fathers (Not Mothers): Their Importance and Influence with Infants and Young Children." *Psychiatry* 39 (1976): 48–53.

Ferri, Elsa. *Growing up in a One-Parent Family*. Atlantic Highlands: Humanities, 1976.

Gilman, Richard C., and Knox, D. "Coping with Fatherhood: The First Year." *Child Psychiatry and Human Development* 6 (Spring 1976): 134–48.

Hamilton, Marshall. *Fathers' Influence on Children*. Chicago: Nelson Hall, 1977.

Herman, William W. "Fathers: What Are You? Who Are You?" *Adolescence* (Spring 1973): 139–49.

Howells, John G. "Fallacies in Child Care II: That Fathering is Unimportant." *ACTA Paedopsychiatrica* 37 (February–March 1970: 3–14.

Knox, David, and Gilman, Richard S. "The First Year of Fatherhood." *Family Perspective* 9 (January 1974): 31–34.

Kossoff, Phyllis. "Parenting: Not for Mothers Only." *American Baby* (June 1978): 12–13.

Kotelchuck, Milton. "The Nature of the Infant's Tie to his Father." Paper presented at the annual meeting of the Society for Research in Child Development, Philadelphia, April 1973.

Kotelchuck, Milton. "The Infant's Relationship to the Father: Experimental Evidence." In *The Role of the Father in Child Development*, edited by Michael E. Lamb. New York: Wiley, 1976.

Lamb, Michael E., ed. *The Role of the Father in Child Development*. New York: Wiley, 1976.

Lamb, Michael E., and Lamb, Jamie E. "The Nature and Importance of the Father-Infant Relationship." *Family Coordinator* 25 (October 1976): 379–85.

Levine, James A. "Redefining the Child Care Problem—Men as Child Nurturers." *Childhood Education* 54 (November–December 1977): 55–61.

Lynn, David B. *The Father: His Role in Child Development*. Monterey: Brooks/Cole, 1974.

Mitchell, George; Redican, Walter K.; and Gomber, John. "Males Can Raise Babies." *Psychology Today* 7 (April 1974): 63–68.

Mussen, Paul, and Distler, Luther. "Masculinity, Identification and Father/Son Relationship." In *Family Roles and Interaction*, edited by Jerold Hess. Chicago: Rand McNally, 1968.

Ostrovaky, Everett S. *Father to the Child*. New York: Putnam & Sons, 1959.

Reiber, Victor D. "Is the Nurturing Role Natural to Fathers?" *American Journal of Maternal Child Nursing* 1 (1976): 86–90.

Taconis, Liba. "The Role of the Contemporary Father in Rearing Young Children." *Educational Research* 11 (February 1969): 83–94.

WORK AND FAMILY

Aberle, David, and Naegele, Kaspar D. "Middle-Class Fathers' Occupational Roles and Attitudes Toward Children." *American Journal of Orthopsychiatry* 22 (April 1952): 366–78.

Aldois, Joan. "Occupational Characteristics and Male Role Performance in the Family." *Journal of Marriage and the Family* 31 (November 1969): 707–12.

Hammel, Lisa. "A Scholarly 'Homemaker-Father' Studies Others Like Himself." *The New York Times,* 14 December 1974, p. 24.

Komarovsky, Mirra. *Dilemmas of Masculinity.* New York: W. W. Norton, 1976.

Oppenheimer, Valerie K. "The Life Cycle Squeeze: The Interaction of Men's Occupational and Family Life Cycles." *Demography* 11 (May 1974): 227–45.

Pleck, Joseph H. "Men's Family Work: Three Perspectives and Some New Data." *Family Coordinator* 28 (October 1979): 126–33.

Raache, Joe. "Confessions of a Househusband." *MS* (November 1972): 10–12.

Veroff, Joel, and Feld, Sheila. *Marriage and Work in America.* New York: Van Nostrand Reinhold, 1970.

FATHER ABSENCE

Aldouse, Joan. "Children's Perspectives of Adult Role Adjustment. Father Absence, Class, Race, and Sex Influence." *Journal of Marriage and the Family* 35 (February 1972): 55–65.

Biller, Henry B. "Father Absence, Maternal Encouragement and Sex-Role Development in Kindergarten Age Boys." *Child Development* 40 (September 1969): 539–46.

Biller, Henry B. "The Mother-Child Relationship and the Father-Absent Boys' Personality Development." *Merrill-Palmer Quarterly* 17 (July 1971): 227–42.

Duberman, Lucille. *The Reconstituted Family: A Study of Remarried Couples and Their Children.* Chicago: Nelson Hall, 1975.

Herzog, Elizabeth, and Sudia, Cecelia E. "Boys in Fatherless Families." U.S. Department of H.E.W., Children's Bureau, 1971, pp. 72–73.

Hetherington, Mavis E. "Effects of Father Absence on Personality Development in Adolescent Daughters." *Developmental Psychology* 7 (November 1973): 313–26.

SINGLE-PARENT FATHERS

Baden-Maratz, Ramona. "Family Form or Process? Reconsidering the Deficit Family Model Approach." *Family Coordinator* 28 (January 1979): 5–14.

Bain, Chris. "Lone Fathers: An Unnoticed Group." *Australian Social Welfare* (March 1973): 142–50.

Bernard, Jessie. *The Future of Marriage.* New York: World Publishers, 1972.

Burgess-Kohn, Jane. "The Single-Parent Family: A Social and Sociological Problem." *Family Coordinator* 19 (1970): 137–44.

Burgess-Kohn, Jane. "The Father's Adjustment as a Single Parent." Paper presented at the annual meeting of the National Council on Family Relations, New York City, October 1976.

Carter, Hugh, and Glick, Paul C. *Marriage and Divorce: A Social and Economic Study*. Cambridge: Harvard University Press, 1970.

Clayton, Peter N. "Meeting the Needs of the Single Parent Family." *Family Coordinator* 20 (1971): 327–36.

Doyle, Richard F. *The Rape of the Male*. St. Paul: Poor Richard's Press, 1976.

Dwyer, Jim. "Behold, the Single Father." *Signature* (September 1974): 81–88.

Fasteau, Marc Feigen. *The Male Machine*. New York: McGraw-Hill, 1974.

Ferri, Elsa. "Characteristics of Motherless Families." *British Journal of Social Work* 3 (Spring 1973): 91–100.

Ferri, Elsa, and Robinson, Hilary. *Coping Alone*. Atlantic Highlands: Humanities, 1977.

Gasser, Rita D., and Taylor, Claribel M. "Role Adjustment of Single Parent Fathers with Dependent Children." *Family Coordinator* 25 (October 1976): 397–400.

George, Victor, and Wilding, Paul. *Motherless Families*. London: Routledge & Kegan Paul, 1973.

Jauch, Carol. "The One-Parent Family." *Journal of Clinical Child Psychology* 6 (Summer 1977): 30–32.

Katz, Arnold J. "Lone Fathers: Perspectives and Implications for Family Policy." *Family Coordinator* 28 (October 1979: 521–29.

Kelly, F. Donald, and Main, Frank O. "Sibling Conflict in a Single-Parent Family: An Empirical Case Study." *American Journal of Family Therapy* 7 (Spring 1979): 39–47.

Keshet, Harry F., and Rosenthal, Kristine M. "Single-Parent Fathers." *Children Today* 7 (May-June 1978): 13–19.

Klein, Carole. "The Single-Parent Male." In *The Single Parent Experience*, pp. 43–59. New York: Avon, 1973.

Lewis, Kenneth. "Single-Father Families: Who They Are and How They Fare." *Child Welfare* 57 (December 1978): 642–51.

McFadden, Michael. *Bachelor Fatherhood: How to Raise and Enjoy Your Children as a Single Parent*. New York: Walker, 1974.

Mendes, Helen A. "Single Fathers." *Family Coordinator* 25 (October 1976): 439–44.

Mendes, Helen A. "Single-Parent Families: A Typology of Life Styles." *Social Work* 24 (May 1978): 193–200.

Meuch, Mervyn. "Motherless Family Project." *British Journal of Social Work* 3 (1973): 363–76.

Molinoff, Daniel. "Life with Father." *New York Times Magazine*, 22 May 1977, p. 12.

Orther, Dennis K.; Brown, Terry; and Ferguson, Dennis. "Single-Parent

Fatherhood: An Emerging Life Style." *Family Coordinator* 25 (October 1976): 429–37.

Savage, J. E. "Community-Social Variables Related to Black Parent-Absent Families." *Marriage and the Family* 40 (November 1978): 779–85.

Schlesinger, Benjamin. "Single Parent Fathers: A Research Review." *Children Today* 7 (May-June 1978): 12.

Schlesinger, Benjamin, and Todres, Rubin. "Motherless Families: An Increasing Social Pattern." *Child Welfare* 55 (October 1976): 553–58.

Schorr, Alvin L., and Moen, Phyllis. "The Single Parent and Public Policy." *Social Policy* 9 (March/April 1979): 15–21.

Stafford, Linley M. *One Man's Family: A Single Father and His Children.* New York: Random House, 1978.

Sullivan, Judy. *Mamma Doesn't Live Here Anymore.* New York: A Fields Books, 1974.

Warner, Nancy J., and Elliot, Carla J. "Problems of the Interpretive Phase of Divorce Custody Evaluations." *Journal of Divorce* 2 (Summer 1979): 371–82.

Warren, Roland L. "Family Maintenance in Father-only Families." Study Project based at Brandeis University, 1976.

Weigard, Jonathan. "The Single Father." In *Readings in Marriage and the Family,* pp. 172–75. Guildford, Conn.: Dushkin Publishing Co., 1974.

Wilding, Paul. "Motherless Families." *New Society,* 24 August 1972, pp. 382–84.

Wilding, Paul. "The Single Father: Learning to Go It Alone." *Sky* (Delta Air Lines), November 1974, pp. 27–29.

Woody, Robert H. "Fathers with Child Custody." *Counseling Psychologist* 7 (April 1978): 60–63.

DIVORCED VISITING FATHERS

Anthony, James. "Children at Risk from Divorce: A Review." In *The Child in His Family: Children at Psychiatric Risk,* edited by E. James Anthony and Cyrille Koupernik. New York: Wiley & Sons, 1974.

Atkin, Edith, and Rubin, Estelle. *Part-Time Father: A Guide for the Divorced Father.* New York: The Vanguard Press, 1977.

Bart, Pauline B. "Divorced Men and Their Children: A Study of Emerging Roles." Paper presented at the annual meeting of the American Sociological Association, Washington, D.C., 1970.

Falligant, Cissi. "If It Ends in Divorce." *Chicago Tribune,* 4 August, 1976, p. 3.

Firth, Raymond, et al. *Families and Their Relatives.* London: Routledge & Kegan Paul, 1970.

Gardner, Richard A. *The Parents' Book About Divorce.* Garden City: Doubleday & Co., 1977.

Hetherington, E. Mavis; Cox, Martha; and Cox, Roger. "Divorced Fathers." *Psychology Today* 10 (April 1977): 417–28.

Hetherington, E. Mavis; Cox, Martha; and Cox, Roger. "The Aftermath of Divorce." In *Mother-Child, Father-Child Relationship*, edited by Joseph H. Sliven and Marilyn Mathews. Washington, D.C.: National Association for Education of Young Children, 1978.

Hunt, Morton. *The World of the Formerly Married*. New York: McGraw-Hill, 1966.

Jacobson, Doris. "The Impact of Marital Separation/Divorce on Child Adjustment." *Journal of Divorce* 1 (Summer 1978): 341–60.

Johnson, Sharon. "Divorced Fathers Organizing to Bolster Role in Children's Lives." *The New York Times*, 7 August 1977, p. 61.

Kelly, Joan B., and Wallerstein, Judith S. "The Effects of Parental Divorce: Experiences of the Child in Early Latency." *American Journal of Orthopsychiatry* 46 (1976): 20–32.

Kelly, Joan B., and Wallerstein, Judith S. "Part-Time Parent, Part-Time Child: Visiting After Divorce." *Journal of Clinical Child Psychology* 6 (1977): 51–54.

Lamb, Michael E. "The Effects of Divorce on Children's Personality Development." *Journal of Divorce* 1 (Winter 1977): 1963–74.

Nye, F. Ivan. "Child Adjustment in Broken and in Unhappy Unbroken Homes." *Marriage and Family Living* 19 (1957): 356–61.

Robinson, Bryan E. "Men Caring for the Young: An Androgynous Perspective." *Family Coordinator* 28 (October 1979): 553–61.

Tessnan, Lora Heins. *Children of Parting Parents*. New York: Jason Aronson, 1978.

Wallerstein, Judith S., and Kelley, Joan B. "The Effects of Parental Divorce: Experiences of the Preschool Child." *Journal of the American Academy of Child Psychiatry* 14 (Autumn 1975): 600–16.

Wallerstein, Judith S., and Kelley, Joan B. "The Effects of Parental Divorce on the Child in Later Latency." *American Journal of Orthopsychiatry* 46 (1976): 256–69.

Wallerstein, Judith S., and Kelley, Joan B. *Surviving the Breakup: How Children and Parents Cope with Divorce*. New York: Basic Books, 1980.

Zeck, Marge. "Divorced Father Must be Many Men." *Minneapolis Tribune*, 19 November 1972, p. 2.

JOINT CUSTODY FATHERS

Abarbanel, A. "Shared Parenting After Separation and Divorce: A Study of Joint Custody." *American Journal of Orthopsychiatry* 49 (April 1979): 329–29.

Abrahams, Sally. "The Joint Custody Controversy." *New York*, 18 June 1979, p. 56.

Baum, Charlotte. "The Best of Both Parents: Joint Custody." *New York Times Magazine*, 31 October 1976, pp. 44–48.

Benedek, Elissa P., and Benedek, Richard S. "Joint Custody: Solution or Illusion?" *American Journal of Psychiatry* 136 (December 1979): 1540–44.

Cox, Mary J., and Cease, Lory. "Joint Custody: What Does it Mean? How Does it Work?" *Family Advocate* (Summer 1978): 10–13.

Dullea, Georgia. "Joint Custody: Is Sharing the Child a Dangerous Idea?" *New York Times,* 24 May 1976, p. 24.

Dullea, Georgia. "Is Joint Custody Good for the Children?" *New York Times Magazine,* 3 February 1980, p. 32.

Equal Custodial Time—A Revolutionary Concept. *Family Law Commentator* 4 (July 1975): 1.

Foster, Henry H., Jr.; Freed, Doris J.; and Grief, Judith B. "Joint Custody." *Trial* 15 (May 1979): 26–33.

Galper, Miriam. "Co-Parenting: Sharing Your Child Equally. A Sourcebook for the Separated or Divorced Family." Philadelphia: Running Press, 1978.

Greif, Judith B. "Father, Children and Joint Custody." *American Journal of Orthopsychiatry* 49 (April 1979): 311–19.

Grote, Douglas F., and Weinstein, Jeff P. "Joint Custody: A Viable and Ideal Alternative." *Journal of Divorce* 1 (Fall 1977): 43–53.

Kay, H., and Phillips, I. "Poverty and the Law of Child Custody." *California Law Review* 717 (1966): 720–32.

Kellog, Mary A. "Joint Custody." *Newsweek,* 24 January 1977, pp. 56–57.

Keshet, Harry F. "Part Time Fathers: A Study of Separated and Divorced Men." Ph.D. dissertation, University of Michigan, 1977.

Keshet, Harry F., and Rosenthal, Kristine M. "Fathering After Marital Separation." *Social Work* 23 (January 1978): 11–18.

Levine, Jo Ann. "Parents Agree to Joint Custody." *Christian Science Monitor,* 5 May 1975, p. 18.

One Child, Two Homes; Joint Custody. *Time,* 29 January 1979), p. 61.

Ornstein, J. Alan. *The Lion's Share.* New York: Times Books, 1978.

Roby, Pamela A. "Shared Parenting: Perspectives from Other Nations." *School Review* (May 1975): 21–24.

Roman, Mel, and Haddad, William. *The Disposable Parent: The Case for Joint Custody.* New York: Holt, Rinehart & Winston, 1978.

Roman, Mel, and Haddad, William. "The Case for Joint Custody." *Psychology Today* 12 (September 1978): 96.

Spock, Benjamin. "Joint Custody and the Father's Role." *Redbook,* October 1979, p. 77.

Ware, Ciji. "Joint Custody: One Way to End the War." *New West,* 26 February 1979, p. 42.

LEGAL RIGHTS OF FATHERS

Aberg, Miriam; Small, Patricia; and Watson, J. Allen. "Males, Fathers and Husbands: Changing Roles and Reciprocal Legal Rights." *Family Coordinator* 26 (October 1977): 287–91.

Bartz, Karen W., and Witcher, Wayne C. "When Father Gets Custody." *Children Today* 7 (Sept-Oct 1978): 2–6, 35.

Behles, Jenny D., and Behles, Daniel J. "Equal Rights in Divorce and Separation." *New Mexico Law Review* 3 (1973): 118–32.

Derdeyn, Andre P. "Child Custody Contests in Historical Perspective." *American Journal of Psychiatry* 133 (December 1976): 1369–76.

Dukette, Robert, and Stevenson, Norman. "The Legal Rights of Unmarried Fathers: The Impact of Recent Court Decisions." *Social Service Review* 47 (January 1973): 1–15.

Ellsworth, Peter, and Levy, Robert. "Legislative Reform and Child Support Adjudication." *Law and Society Review* 4 (November 1970): 166–225.

Foster, Henry H., Jr. "Adoption and Child Custody: Best Interests of the Child?" *Buffalo Law Review* 22 (Fall 1972): 1–16.

Goldstein, Joseph; Freud, Anna; and Solnit, Albert J. *Beyond the Best Interests of the Child.* New York: Free Press, 1973.

Quinn, Susan. "Fathers Cry for Custody." *Juris Doctor* (May 1976): 42.

Roth, Allan. "The Tender Years Presumption in Child Custody Disputes." *Journal of Family Law* 3 (1976–77): 423–62.

Salk, Lee. "On the Custody Rights of Fathers in Divorce." *Journal of Clinical Child Psychology* 6 (Summer 1977): 49–50.

Solomon, Peter F. "Fathers' Revolution in Custody Cases." *Trial* 13 (October 1977): 32–37.

Stack, Carol B. "Who Owns the Child? Divorce and Child Custody Decisions in Middle-Class Families." *Social Problems* 33 (April 1979): 505–15.

Van Gelder, Lawrence. "New Custody Customs: In the Best Interests of the Child." *The New York Times,* 30 October 1976, p. 38.

Victor, Ira, and Winkler, William A. *Father and Custody.* New York: Hawthorn, 1977.

Watson, Andrew. "The Children of Armageddon: Problems of Custody Following Divorce." *Syracuse Law Review* 21 (Fall 1969): 231–39.

Index

181